TOWARD REUNION

D0920132

TOWARD REUNION

*The Roman Catholic
and the Orthodox Churches*

by
Edward J. Kilmartin, S.J.

PAULIST PRESS
New York/Ramsey/Toronto

Copyright © 1979 by
Edward J. Kilmartin, S.J.

All rights reserved. No part of this book may be reproduced or transmitted in any
form or by any means, electronic or mechanical, including photocopying, recording or
by any information storage and retrieval system without permission in writing from
the Publisher.

Library of Congress
Catalog Card Number: 79-88570

ISBN: 0-8091-2236-7

Published by Paulist Press
Editorial Office: 1865 Broadway, New York, N.Y. 10023
Business Office: 545 Island Road, Ramsey, N.J. 07446

Printed and bound in the
United States of America

Contents

v

To
Archbishop Iakovos,
on the occasion of the
twentieth anniversary of his enthronement
as Greek Orthodox Primate of the Americas,
and to all my brothers
of the Orthodox-Roman Catholic Consultation

Preface

Among the most important events within the ecumenical movement since 1960 must be counted the change in official relations between the Orthodox and Roman Catholic Churches. No less significant has been the increasingly sympathetic attitude of many prominent theologians of both churches toward doctrinal differences long considered irreconcilable. In a certain sense, the first chapter of this modern history of Orthodox-Roman Catholic relations reached its climax in 1975 with the announcement of the intention of both churches to begin an international dialogue and closed in 1978 with the convening of the Joint Coordinating Group to draw up a concrete plan for the official dialogue.

Understandably, no comprehensive account of these developments has been written. Neither does there exist an adequate overview of the more important aspects of this changing situation. This book is intended to respond to the latter need. It is limited to a discussion of the more significant decisions taken at the level of the international hierarchy of both churches, the unique dialogue being conducted at the level of the national hierarchy in the U.S.A. and the progress being made toward the resolution of certain major doctrinal differences between Orthodox and Roman Catholic theology.

The material presented here was first offered in a workshop at Notre Dame Seminary, New Orleans, La., October 20-22, 1978. The enthusiastic response accorded the author provided the stimulus to rewrite the lectures for publication.

Introduction

In the late 20th century the leadership of the Orthodox and Roman Catholic Churches has shown a lively interest in forging closer ties with one another. The hope is even expressed that the schism which has continued for many centuries can be healed. This is ultimately based on the claim of these churches that their doctrine and practice conform to those of the ancient Patriarchates of Constantinople and Rome which lived in full communion in the first millennium. During that period these patriarchates shared a common faith openly and defended it together in general councils. They extended the service of brotherly love to one another and confessed the grounds of their unity liturgically by giving each other the one bread and the one cup of the Lord's Supper.

The first chapter of this book outlines the history of the relations between these churches from their origins up through the period when they gradually drifted apart. It also traces certain changes which occurred in the Orthodox Church since that period. With this background, the reader is in a better position to understand the following two chapters.

The subject of the second chapter is the modern Orthodox-Roman Catholic dialogue at the level of national churches. It is necessarily limited to a report on the official dialogue between the Standing Conference of Canonical Orthodox Bishops of America (SCOBA) and the United States Conference of Catholic Bishops' Committee for Ecumenical Affairs (BCEIA) which is carried on by means of a bilateral commission. No counterpart to this dialogue exists elsewhere in the world.

The third chapter traces the recent history of contacts between the two churches at the international level which resulted in the establishment of the international Inter-Orthodox and Roman Catholic Theological Commissions to prepare for dialogue. The achievements of these two commissions over the past two years are summarized and observations are made on the subject matter assigned for the first phase of the work of the bilateral commission.

The final chapter focuses on some doctrinal issues which have been considered serious obstacles to reunion. Traditionally these center around the divergent approaches to the subject of the Triune God and the church. In the former case these themes have occasioned the greatest difficulties: (1) knowledge of God; (2) mission of the Holy Spirit to the church; (3) procession of the Holy Spirit within the Trinity. Among the outstanding ecclesiological problems are: (1) the nature of a general council of the church; (2) the Petrine Office. All these subjects are discussed from the viewpoint of modern Roman Catholic theology. Contributions within this confessional theology have produced encouraging results. Above all, from this standpoint, the differences in Trinitarian doctrine appear less formidible. The two ecclesiological questions are another matter. Yet even here recent developments offer some hope that the impasse may be overcome.

1.

History of Orthodox-Roman Catholic Relations

Why is a fruitful dialogue between the Orthodox and Roman Catholic Churches possible? What constitutes a major difficulty which stands in the way of beginning a common quest for ecclesiastical communion? A response to the first question involves a consideration of the history of relations between the two churches up to the time of the schism and an account of the cause of the schism. To answer the second question reference must be made to the structural changes which have taken place in the Orthodox Church since the schism.

The first part of this chapter describes the early relations between the two churches which provide the basis for the hope that they may now be able to view their differences in a new light. On the one hand, they lived in communion with one another for centuries and have preserved the essentials which made that communion possible. On the other hand, the growing estrangement can be traced to the political situation and ecclesiastical self-serving. In this climate cultural differences and different styles of ecclesiastical life were accentuated. These differences had always existed but by the 9th century they presented formidable hindrances to union in the wake of a more fundamental personal alienation. This history points to the conclusion that what is needed, no more and no less, is a dialogue in love.

The subject of the second part of this chapter is the

evolution of the internal structure of the Orthodox Church. At the time of the schism the Patriarch of Constantinople exercised actual jurisdiction over the whole of Orthodoxy. Consequently, the Orthodox Church presented a unified front in negotiations with the Patriarch of the West. Now there are several churches which are jurisdictionally independent. Moreover, the Moscow Patriarchate has emerged as a second center of Orthodoxy, comparable to Constantinople. The multiplication of autocephalous, or independent churches in the climate of growing national consciousness has occasioned a certain tension which must be overcome before the Orthodox national churches can really speak together as one church with Rome.

An important structural change has also taken place in the Roman Catholic Church during the second millennium. It has to do with the collapse of the concept of universal church as a communion of local churches. The emergence of a centralistic view and practice of the unity of the church in which the power of jurisdiction, understood in the widest sense possible, was concentrated in Rome is a source of great difficulty for the Orthodox. This problem is treated in the final chapter. It is not taken up here because this style of exercise of authority does not hinder the Roman Catholic Church from beginning a serious dialogue with the Orthodox. On the contrary it enables this church to speak with a unified voice.

In the final section of this chapter a survey is given of the history of the Orthodox Church in North America. This information enables the reader to get a better grasp of the peculiar situation which exists in the relationships between the various Orthodox jurisdictions in the U.S.A. Hence it provides the necessary background for the subsequent discussion of the Orthodox-Roman Catholic dialogue in this country. Where these jurisdictions stand with respect to one another determines the extent of present possibilities for improving relations between the Orthodox and Roman Catholic Churches in the U.S.A.

1. History of Orthodox-Roman Catholic Relations on the International Level

The Christian Church had its original center in Jerusalem. From there Christians went north and established a second center at Antioch before A.D. 40. From Jerusalem and Syria a Christian migration to Rome founded a community there before A.D. 43. To the south, Palestinian Christians founded a fourth center at Alexandria very early.

While Jerusalem faded as an important center of Christianity, the Christian communities at Rome, Antioch and Alexandria continued to grow in prominence. The churches of these major cities of the Roman Empire served as mother churches for those which they established in surrounding territories. Their bishops were considered focal points of unity of the regional churches. In addition, the Roman bishop was regarded as already exercising a special role in the service of the unity of the church in the third century.

After the Ecumenical Council of Nicaea, 325, the three patriarchal centers were increased to five. In the 4th century, Constantinople became the capital of the new empire. The second ecumenical council was held there in 381 and granted to its church the status of second patriarchate. Finally at the fourth ecumenical council, held at Chalcedon in 451, Jerusalem was made a patriarchate because of its historical importance.

At the Council of Chalcedon, the dogma of the unity of the humanity and divinity in Christ was affirmed in language which was unacceptable to several segments of the Eastern patriarchates. They drifted off into schism. The churches derived from them, called Oriental Churches, remain in communion with one another but not with Rome or Constantinople. Among these, which often take the name of Orthodox or Apostolic, are counted the Armenian, Coptic, Ethiopian, Indian Malabar and Syrian Churches. At present they are engaged in dialogue with both Rome and Constantinople.

After the unfortunate affair of schism occasioned by Chalcedon, the Patriarchates of Constantinople and Rome continued to live in communion for many centuries. They held three more general councils which are recognized by both churches as ecumenical, the last being the Second Ecumenical Council of Nicaea, 787. However, during the period from the 9th to the 11th centuries, due in great part to political factors, they became more and more estranged from one another. The loss of ordinary contact accentuated the differences in their styles of life. Each found difficulties with the peculiar practices of the other. For example, the Byzantine Church deplored recent Latin innovations in the liturgy, while the Latin Church was extremely critical of the Byzantine practice of allowing married clergy. No remedy could be found to halt the growing alienation which finally led to a confrontation and the disasterous decisions of two ecclesiastics ill-equipped for delicate negotiations. The whole affair of the "Anathemas of 1054" can be quickly summarized.

In the 11th century, Norman Latin Catholics conquered provinces of southern Italy which were under the jurisdiction of the Byzantine emperor, Constantine IX. Rome then forced the Byzantine churches to come under the control of Latin bishops. The Patriarch of Constantinople, Michael Cerularius, retaliated by forcing Greek practices on the Latin churches in Constantinople. In the same year, 1053, he persuaded Leo of Ochrida, head of the Bulgarian Church, to write a letter to John, bishop of Trani, representative of the patriarchate in southern Italy. John gave this letter, critical of a number of Latin usages, to the papal secretary, Humbert. He, in turn, delivered it to Pope Leo IX who was under house arrest by the Normans.

The pope ordered Humbert to write letters to Leo of Ochrida and Cerularius stressing papal primacy and another, with no addressee named, defending Latin usages. Before these letters could be sent, two others arrived from the East. The Byzantine emperor requested closer political ties; Cerularius expressed his desire for better relations and promised to return the pope's name to the diptychs, removed since 1019.

In the meantime Pope Leo was steadily failing in health, a condition brought on in great part by his physical participation in the campaign against the Normans. Negotiations had to be put in the hands of Humbert. Under orders from the pope he headed a delegation which was instructed to settle the differences in Constantinople. Arriving in April 1054, the papal secretary and the other two legates were well received by the emperor. Cerularius, suspicious of its credentials, steadfastly refused to meet with the papal delegation. As summer wore on the frustrated Humbert finally made a fateful move which suited the plan of Cerularius, known from two letters to Peter of Antioch, to lead the Orthodox Church into schism and to show the Latins to be heretics.

On July 16, 1054 the papal delegation went to the Hagia Sophia at the time of the Divine Liturgy and placed a bull of excommunication on the main altar. It was directed against Cerularius, Leo of Ochrida and Constantine, the chancellor of Cerularius. After reading a translation of the text Cerularius summoned the permanent synod which anathematized the document and the authors. No mention is made of the Pope of Rome, who had died on April 19, 1054, or the Roman Church.

It is evident that the two anathemas were not the cause of the schism between the East and West. Still it cannot be denied that they provided ammunition for those who were intent on dividing the church. A more serious ground for the rupture must be attributed to the Latin crusaders who conquered Constantinople in 1204. On this occasion a Latin Patriarch was installed and the Eastern Patriarch was forced to retreat to Nicaea until the recapture of the city. The embitterment resulting from this hostile act was enough in itself to undermine any attempt of the West to reestablish ordinary relations with the Patriarch of Constantinople in the foreseeable future. However, the West made the effort at the Second Council of Lyons in 1274. This failed as did the later attempt at the Council of Florence, 1439-1445. Since then Rome and Constantinople have lived in a state of separation from one another.

An additional source of antagonism between the two churches resulted from Rome's decision, since the schism, to enter into communion with segments of the churches historically linked to Constantinople. This is especially true where overt proselytism was involved but also in cases where the initiative did not come from Rome. These communities, together with the segments of the Oriental Churches which have reunited with Rome, are called Eastern Catholics by the West and Uniates by the East. They retain the name of the church from which they derive historically as well as their ancient liturgy and canon law. The existence of these churches within countries which are traditionally Orthodox is still an ongoing source of tension between Rome and Constantinople.

2. Structural Changes in the Orthodox Church

After the separation from the Latin Church the Patriarchs of Constantinople continued to exercise a form of jurisdictional primacy over the whole of Orthodoxy. But their claim to this role, based on Canon 28 of the Council of Chalcedon, gradually eroded wtih the decay of the political influence which they had gained through the Byzantine emperors and later through the Ottoman Empire. The more recent awakening of national consciousness and the formation of national states led to a further limitation of the Ecumenical Patriarch's direct jurisdiction and his recognition of the autocephalous status of the churches of Greece, Serbia and

Romania in the 19th century, and the churches of Georgia, Poland, Albania and Bulgaria in the 20th century.

Further loss of influence of Constantinople over Orthodoxy was occasioned by the Russian Revolution. In this upheaval, two important changes took place which affected the Russian Orthodox Church's view of itself. First of all, beginning in 1920, when the remnants of the White Army fled, a migration of large numbers of Russian Orthodox clergy and laity to all parts of the world took place. Second, shortly after the Communist Party gained control of the government in 1917 all property, including that belonging to the church, was nationalized and this act was followed at the outset of the new year with "The Decree on the Separation of the Church from the State and of School from the Church."

In the 17th century, Czar Peter I had refused to allow the election of a patriarch after the see became vacant. Instead he appointed a Chief Procurator as direct representative of the czar in the governing synod. Thus a state church was born. This situation continued until the decree on separation of church from state which provided the opportunity for the convocation of a Pan-Russian Church Council and the restoration of the patriarchate. The council met in 1917/1918 and elected Tikhon, Metropolitan of Moscow, as patriarch.

With this decision the Russian Orthodox Church as a whole gained a new self-understanding of its independent status not only with respect to the state but within Orthodoxy. Moreover, the world-wide diaspora, with which it was related as mother church, gave it a new sense of catholicity.

The Moscow patriarchate has become quite conscious of itself as an Orthodox center with a global reach. This is concretely manifested by certain of its unilateral decisions which, in the normal course of events would seem to require the consent of all the autocephalous churches of Orthodoxy. For example, it granted autocephalous status to the Russian Orhhodox Greek Catholic Church of America in 1970 which now takes the title: The Orthodox Church of America. This was done without the consent of the Patriarch of Constantinople who still does not recognize the juridical validity of this act. Moreover, the new name could be construed as a direct challenge to the authority of the Patriarch of Constantinople who exercises jurisdiction over the Greek Orthodox Archdiocese in the U.S.A. It seems to imply that Moscow gives its blessing to other Orthodox jurisdictions to join this autocephalous church.

The emergence of two centers of Orthodoxy in this century requires that the Orthodox Church find a way to do justice to this new situation. It is recognized by all parties concerned that this can only be done through a Pan-Orthodox Council. The need for such a meeting of all autocephalous Orthodox Churches to discuss and arrive at common decisions about a variety of pastoral and jurisdictional problems was recognized by the Ecumenical patriarchate after the First World War. Several times Constantinople attempted to convene a Pan-Orthodox Conference to prepare for a general council. This first step was finally taken mainly through the efforts of Patriarch Athenagoras I of Constantinople. He was able to organize and bring about a meeting of all autocephalous churches at Rhodes in 1961. Since that time considerable progress has been made in the preparation for a "Great and Holy Council" of the Orthodox Church.

The meetings of the Pan-Orthodox Conference are treated in more detail in chapter III. However, it should be noted here that these meetings afforded the opportunity for the Orthodox Church to discuss the question of ecumenical relations with the Roman Catholic Church. Stimulated by the openness of the Second Vatican Council to the Orthodox Church and the friendly personal exchanges between Patriarch Athenagoras I and Pope Paul VI, the Pan-Orthodox Conference decided in favor of preparing for official theological dialogue with Rome. In the last few years, relations between the two churches have so improved that a further step became possible. In 1975 Inter-Orthodox and Roman Catholic commissions were established to make concrete preparations for this dialogue. A more extended account of these negotiations is also found in chapter III.

3. History of the Orthodox Church in North America

The first significant Orthodox presence in North America dates back to July 15, 1741 when Russian explorers, John Bering and Alexis Chirikov, discovered the coast of Alaska. Five days later a priest accompanying the expedition celebrated the first Orthodox Divine Liturgy in North America aboard the ship St. Peter.

During the next fifty years Russian fur traders and fishermen journeyed back and forth to Alaska operating out of temporary settlements. A village was finally founded in 1784 near present-day Kodiak. Ten years later a church was opened here by eight monks who began to evangelize the natives. One of them, Fr. Herman worked with the Aleuts for forty-three years. He was canonized in 1970 by the Orthodox Church of America shortly after it received autocephalous status from Moscow.

The attempt in 1798 to establish a missionary bishopric in Alaska failed when one of the original monks, returning from Russia after episcopal consecration, was drowned in a shipwreck. The first Russian Orthodox bishop to work in the territory was John Veniaminov. He had been an Alaskan missionary. In 1840 he was consecrated Bishop Innocent of the new see Kamchatka, North East Siberia, which included the Alaskan mission headquartered at Sitka.

In 1858 the bishopric of Sitka was established as an auxiliary see to the Kamchatka diocese. After the sale of

Alaska to the U.S.A. (1867) Sitka became an independent missionary see in 1870. Two years later the bishop's see was transferred to San Francisco and in 1900 it received the title Diocese of the Aleutian Islands and North America. The see was again moved five years later to New York City where it has remained.

The other currently most influential representative of the Orthodox Church in the U.S.A. is the Greek Orthodox Church. The history of Greek Orthodox in North America shows that they were the first among the Orthodox to establish a community on American soil, at New Smyrna, Florida in 1767. They also founded the first parish within the territory of the U.S.A., Holy Trinity at New Orleans in 1864. Moreover, while the main current of immigration of Russian Orthodox to the U.S.A. began after the First World War, the number of Greek Orthodox immigrants between 1900-1921 probably matched that of all other countries combined. As a result, Greek Orthodox parishes numbered 130 by 1918. But they were not well organized. Some were under the jurisdiction of the Russian diocese, others were loosely affiliated with the Patriarch of Constantinople.

This situation was remedied by Archbishop Meletios Metaxakis who was forced to leave Athens for political reasons. Arriving in the U.S.A. in 1920 he began to organize the parishes under the jurisdiction of the Synod of Athens of which he still considered himself the head. This was made easy because the one canonical representative at the episcopal level was the Russian Orthodox Church. But because of the Russian Revolution the Moscow Patriarch was unable to exercise effective control.

In the next year Metaxakis was elected Patriarch of Constantinople and in that capacity formally transferred the Greek Orthodox Archdiocese of America from the jurisdiction of Athens to that of Constantinople in 1922.

As a result of the activity of Metaxakis, for the first time in history, different Orthodox ecclesiastical jurisdictions appeared within the same geographical area. This paved the way for one national Orthodox Church after another to establish its own jurisdiction in the U.S.A.

The proximity of these jurisdictions to one another did not tend initially to foster cooperation in matters of common concern. However, the Standing Conference of Canonical Orthodox Bishops of America was established in 1960 in order to promote communication between the overlapping jurisdictions. It has been successful in dealing with some internal problems of the Orthodox Church in the U.S.A. It has also entered into dialogue with the Anglican, Lutheran, Reformed and Roman Catholic Churches. The last named has proved to be the most fruitful of all the dialogues in which SCOBA is involved. Its history and achievements provide the subject matter of the next chapter.

However, SCOBA did not find an answer to the problem of the divisions of Orthodoxy in the U.S.A. which suited the Russian diocese. Since this diocese declared itself a temporarily self-administrative metropolia in 1924, until normal relations could be resumed with Moscow, it has been struggling to maintain its identity as an American church. Within SCOBA it has argued for the establishment of the identity and unity of American Orthodoxy for several years.

Unsatisfied with the response it received, the Russian diocese entered into negotiations with Moscow and received autocephalous status in 1970. It has thus become the only completely self-governing American Orthodox Church affiliated with SCOBA. This new situation has only increased the strained relations within the various jurisdictions. The Greek Orthodox archdiocese is especially disappointed because in its eyes the authority of the Patriarch of Constantinople has been ignored. In its judgment he should have been a party to the decision made by Moscow. Together with the Patriarch of Constantinople, the Greek archdiocese does not recognize the independent status of the Orthodox Church of America and continues to refer to it as the Russian Orthodox Greek Catholic Church in America.

This particular internal problem of the Orthodox Church in the U.S.A. provides the single most serious obstacle to cooperation between the various jurisdictions both with respect to resolving internal ecclesiastical difficulties and presenting a unified voice in the dialogue with other churches.

2.
The Orthodox-Roman Catholic Dialogue in the U.S.A.

The Standing Conference of Canonical Orthodox Bishops of America and the United States Conference of Catholic Bishops' Committee for Ecumenical Affairs established a bilateral consultative body in 1965. The Roman Catholic Church had committed itself to such dialogues in the Second Vatican Council's *Decree on Ecumenism*, no. 18, issued on November 21, 1964. The Pan-Orthodox Conference opened the way to Orthodox involvement in its decision, taken in 1964 at III Rhodes, which approved "informal dialogue" with other Christian churches.

This bilateral commission was mandated to explore theological issues and pastoral problems of common concern to both churches with a view to removing obstacles to full ecclesiastical communion. Since its inception it has met nineteen times at this writing. The first meeting took place in Worcester, Mass., September 5, 1965; the last meeting was held in New York, N.Y., December 7-8, 1978. Archbishop Iakovos, head of the Greek Orthodox archdiocese of North and South America and chairman of SCOBA, has been the Orthodox Church chairman from the outset. Currently William Cardinal Baum, Archbishop of Washington, D.C., is the Roman Catholic chairman. He succeeded Bishop Bernard Flanagan of the Diocese of Worcester, Mass., who held the post until 1973. The remainder of the membership includes Scripture scholars,

17

theologians, canon lawyers, liturgiologists and historians. They have been drawn mainly from the Greek and Russian Orthodox and Roman Catholic Churches. For some time an equal representation of Greek and Russian scholars attended the meeting. But since the establishment of the Orthodox Church of America the Russian representation has been minimal.

The commission has dealt with numerous theological and pastoral problems. It has issued seven consensus statements of a doctrinal nature and two other communications. The consensus statements are the following: (1) *An Agreed Statement on the Holy Eucharist*; (2) *An Agreed Statement on Mixed Marriages*; (3) *An Agreed Statement on Respect for Life;* (4) *An Agreed Statement on the Church*; (5) *The Pastoral Office: A Joint Statement*; (6) *The Principle of Economy: A Joint Statement*; (7) *An Agreed Statement on the Sanctity of Marriage*. The texts of these statements are found in I Appendix.

The first communication took the form of a memorandum concerning the agenda of the Pre-Synodal Pan-Orthodox Conference which was proposed for the forthcoming Great and Holy Council. The second was a letter addressed to the President of the U.S.A. and the Secretary of State concerning the persecution of the Greek Orthodox community in Turkey. These documents are found in I Appendix.

A complete discussion of the work of this commission exceeds the boundaries of this volume. We will consider only (1) the main findings of the commission concerning doctrinal agreement and differences which constitute obstacles to reunion of the churches; (2) the approach to certain pastoral problems which, in the judgment of the commission, can be alleviated more easily, and in some cases only by the cooperative effort of both churches.

Initially the commission discussed two subjects which were quickly shelved. It recognized the need for cooperation in the continuing education of the clergy and laity of both churches concerning the beliefs and practices of their sister church. No concrete proposals were forthcoming. But it is recognized that this subject will have to be taken up again since it provides an indispensable means of promoting fellowship among the Orthodox and Roman Catholic clergy and laity.

A consideration of the differences between Orthodox and Roman Catholic theological methods also terminated very soon. There seems to have been an implicit agreement that different ways of theologizing are found in both Orthodox and Roman Catholic circles. Moreover, as a whole, the commission admitted the value of certain modern methods of biblical exegetes, systematic theologians and historians and used them to good advantage in the investigation of doctrinal and pastoral problems.

The doctrinal questions which received most attention were the theology of the Eucharist, church, pastoral office and marriage. Pastoral problems, which the commission investigated, centered around themes related to marriage. A summary and evaluation of the work of the commission in these areas constituted the remainder of this chapter.

1. Mass—Divine Liturgy

The agreed statements on Eucharist, church and pastoral office confirm the scholarly opinion that traditional Orthodox and Roman Catholic understandings of the Mass or Divine Liturgy, as the Orthodox call it, agree on essentials. Underlying the different theological approaches to the eucharistic mystery there is a consensus concerning the following:

A. *The meaning of the Eucharist*: The celebration expresses and realizes the mystery of the acceptable worship of Christ and the church and so is source of blessings for the living and the dead. Through the celebration, the bread and cup become sacrament of the saving presence of the risen Lord and spiritually benefit the believing communicant.

B. *The relation of Eucharist to church*: As the most profound liturgical expression of the mystery of church, this celebration manifests and realizes the church most perfectly according to the measure of devotion of the participants.

C. *The requirement of pastoral office*: As an essential element of the structure of the local church the leadership of pastoral office (= bishop or presbyter) is required for the celebration of this sacrament which most perfectly manifests and realizes church.

D. *The requirement for common eucharistic worship*: Since the celebration is the most perfect manifestation and realization of church, it supposes a unity of the participants that covers the whole range of the essentials of the life of the church.

The *Agreed Statement on the Holy Eucharist* omits mention of the differing Orthodox and Roman Catholic approaches to the theology of consecration. Eastern theology commonly focuses on the consecratory function of the invocation of the Holy Spirit (=*epiclesis*). Western theology highlights the role of the recitation of the account of institution of the Eucharist by the priest. Furthermore, this agreed statement prescinds partially from the differing approaches to the explanation of the nature of the transformation of the bread and wine by which they become sacrament of Christ's personal presence. Eastern theology generally refers to the transforming power of the Spirit who modifies the relationships of things and persons to the glorified Lord. Thus, through the Spirit, the elements become source of the personal presence of Christ "for us." The nature of the transformation is not discussed further. Western theology traditionally adds a philosophical explanation that attempts to describe more precisely what happens to the physical elements: the theory of transubstantiation.

In the judgment of the commission, the varying theological approaches to the relationship between the epiclesis and the account of institution lie outside the scope of that affirmation of faith which is a condition for eucharistic sharing between the two churches. Concerning the nature of the transformation of the bread and wine, the commission is agreed that the theory of transubstantiation takes as point of departure the dogma of the transforming action of the Spirit but does not pertain to the scope of what must be believed about Christ's sacramental presence. It is not necessary to accept this theory in order to maintain the unity of faith of the undivided church.

Finally, the way in which the commission explains the requirement of liturgical leadership of bishop or presbyter for a true Eucharist shows that it does not consider the medieval interpretations of the priest's power of consecration to pertain to the essentials of eucharistic faith. More patristically, liturgically and ecclesiologically orientated, the *Agreed Statement on Pastoral Office* grounds this necessity on the fact that the local church has the essential structure of the ordained minister in apostolic succession and community which lives by apostolic faith. This structure should be concretely manifested in the eucharistic celebration which most perfectly manifests and realizes the church of Christ "in every place."

2. Church

The commission has paid special attention to the problem of the reciprocal recognition of the ecclesial status of the Orthodox and Roman Catholic Churches. It is agreed that one must speak of degrees of membership in the church both at the level of each local community and at the level of the communion of local churches. Not every member of a local church participates equally in the mystery of the church. Some live deeper lives of faith than others. Correspondingly not every church, as a whole, participates in the fullness of the apostolic tradition. Heretical churches: those which select elements of the whole tradition and reject others, are a fact of life.

In principle both the Orthodox and Roman Catholic Churches consider that the fullness of the apostolic tradition is found in their respective communities. Hence both ask: To what extent can one recognize the ecclesial status of the other? *The Principle of Economy: A Joint Statement* records the present thinking of the commission on this issue. It refers to the need for the exercise of discernment. Hence it calls for a continued effort of both churches to seek to discover the basis for recognition of each other as "sister churches" and so celebrants of the same sacraments.

An Agreed Statement on the Church provides a clue to one of the major difficulties preventing mutual recognition. This document focuses on the local church. Taking as point of departure the mystery of the Trinity, it argues that the church finds its prototype there. In the Trinity there is both distinction of persons and unity based on love. The church should reflect this plurality and unity based on love not external law.

The continuity of the church with its origins is thus grounded on the source of love in the church: the Holy Spirit. The active presence of the Spirit is described as finding its visible expression in such historical forms as Scripture, the sacraments and ministry ordained in apostolic succession. Since these historical forms are found in the concrete local church, the community gathered around its bishop and other ministers is truly church. The independent existence of the local church is considered best expressed in the eucharistic celebration where the church most profoundly manifests and realizes itself. At the same time the local church is viewed as interdependent in relation to other churches which possess the same Spirit of Christ.

Within the interdependence of local churches a hierarchy is recognized which does not exclude a fundamental equality of all churches. At this point the document refers to the different Orthodox and Roman Catholic explanations of the primacy in the church which constitutes a major obstacle to reunion.

As the document shows, the commission has not been able, as a whole, to offer any positive suggestions to resolve the opposing views. It takes for granted that a solution can be found since the Orthodox and Roman Catholic Churches lived in communion with one another for the first millennium. However, the Orthodox Church rejects the First Vatican Council's version of the primacy of the Roman Patriarch over the universal church in matters of doctrine and jurisdiction. A form of primacy is acceptable to the Orthodox but, at least in theory, it is not automatically attached to any particular patriarchate. Currently it is considered to be linked to the Patriarchate of Constantinople. In addition, this primacy is not awarded the all-embracing jurisdictional and teaching authority attributed to the Pope in Rome by Roman Catholics.

The question of primacy in the church has also been discussed by the commission in connection with the theology of ecumenical councils. Here the theme of the infallibility of the church was raised. Again the commission has not been able to provide a commonly agreed on statement to help solve the irreconcilable positions of the Orthodox and Roman Catholic Churches. The Orthodox refuse to situate infallibility completely within any structure of the ministry, even of a general council of the church. The teaching expressed by the episcopacy within a general council of the church or by the whole episcopacy outside a council cannot be considered ultimately binding on the faithful until it has been received by the whole church. It needs confirmation by the whole church before it is recognized as object of the assent of saving faith.

This position is opposed to the official position of the Roman Catholic Church which holds that the teaching office of the church, in the person of the bishop of Rome as head of the episcopal college, or in the form of a general council with the bishop of Rome as head, can make dogmatic statements which are from the moment of their solemn pronouncement to be considered as infallible statements of saving faith which ultimately bind the believer.

3. Pastoral Office

As *The Pastoral Office: A Joint Statement* shows, there are few issues on which the two churches differ in their understanding of the office exercised by bishops and presbyters. The outstanding difference is the interpretation of the Petrine office. The commission notes, however, that an important development has taken place in unofficial Roman Catholic circles: The seemingly widespread consensus that women are qualified for episcopal and presbyteral ordination.

This same document also touches on the style of life of pastors. It affirms that those engaged in the pastoral ministry should not be excluded automatically from occupations which are not directly related to it. The contrary opinion is judged not to have sufficient basis in traditional practice or in the theology of pastoral office. The commission is, therefore, open to the view that presbyters or bishops can engage in public secular office, etc.

The relation of celibacy to the episcopate and presbyterate presents a problem for both churches. Both maintain the ideal of the celibate bishop or presbyter. The Orthodox Church does this by insisting that a priest who marries after ordination may not continue to exercise his ministry and by allowing only unmarried men to be ordained bishops. The Latin rite of the Roman Catholic Church promotes this ideal by not allowing married men to be ordained to the presbyterate except in rare cases. For example, a convert Reformation

Church minister who desires to become a Catholic priest is sometimes ordained, at least conditionally, even though he is married.

The agreed statement simply notes that (1) the question of marriage after presbyteral ordination and the eligibility of married priests for the episcopacy is being discussed in the Orthodox Church; (2) the celibacy issue in the Latin rite centers on the advisability of ordaining married men to the presbyterate.

4. Christian Marriage

Over the years the subject of Christian marriage has occupied most of the attention of the commission. It was studied under the following headings: (1) the sacramental nature of Christian marriage; (2) indissolubility of Christian marriage; (3) role of the liturgical leader in the marriage rite; (4) marriages between Orthodox and Roman Catholics; (5) pastoral care of the divorced and those experiencing failure in the marital state; (6) ethical issues related to marriage.

The subject of indissolubility of Christian marriage and the role of the priest in the marriage rite fall within the scope of the more general theme of the sacramental nature of Christian marriage. These questions are raised because both churches affirm the sacramental nature of marriage between Christians.

The discussion about the sacrament of marriage resulted in *An Agreed Statement on the Sanctity of Marriage*. Here it is stated that both churches agree on the following: In Christian marriage this particular human situation is taken up into the life of faith. As a consequence, the marriage partners engage themselves in a permanent commitment to share fully their lives with one another. The sealing of this commitment takes place in an ecclesial context in which the partners are strengthened in the measure of their response of faith to fulfill their marital vows through the presence of Christ in the Spirit. They are given the grace, which must be continually responded to in faith, to live the type of relationship which exists between Christ and the church (Eph. 5:31-35) and so to witness to each other and to the world this enduring love of God for the world.

Within this perspective, which highlights the missionary task of the couple, the subject of divorce and remarriage is treated. Under certain conditions the Orthodox traditionally permit divorce and tolerate remarriage even in the case of a consummated sacramental marriage. They do this in the interest of forestalling further human tragedies. The Roman Catholic Church recognizes that, for weighty reasons, sacramental marriages which have not been consummated can be dissolved. But in its present official theology and practice, which has a long tradition, it does not recognize true divorce with the possibility of remarriage in the case of consummated sacramental marriages.

The two traditional approaches to the permanency of a consummated sacramental marriage are not reconcilable. While taking this for granted the commission has not yet begun a prolonged study to discover whether the impasse provides a permanent obstacle to ecclesial communion between the churches or whether it might be overcome by a reconsideration of both traditions.

When this study begins it is recognized that the theological significance of four important historical facts will have to be considered. First of all, the Orthodox Church has never formally and officially accused the Roman Catholic Church of an error in its teaching about the indissolubility of a consummated sacramental marriage. On the other hand, the 24th session of the Council of Trent only anathematized those who accused the Roman Catholic Church of erring in its teaching on this matter. Canon 7 of this session was purposely worded in this way to exclude the Greeks who had another opinion but did not accuse the Latin Church of error. Second, neither the Council of Trent nor any other general council of the Roman Catholic Church, nor a pope has declared the bond of consummated sacramental marriages to be indissoluble in a solemn declaration considered by Catholics to be an infallible statement of saving faith. Third, the Latin Church has lived with both the Orthodox illicity tradition (= the first marriage is a fragile union in need of special care; to break it and remarry is against the will of God and gravely illicit) and the invalidity tradition (= the first consummated marriage is indissoluble; the second attempt is invalid while the partners of the first marriage are living) beyond the first millennium.

Pope Gregory II, in a letter written to St. Boniface in 726, even allows that it is licit for a man whose wife has contracted an infirmity which prevents sexual intercourse to remarry if he cannot live chastely. Pope Alexander III disagreed with this viewpoint in a letter of uncertain date written during his papacy (1159-1181). He considers a legitimate marital consent to be an obstacle to a licit second marriage. He does not say that the second marriage would be invalid. Still by requiring that the partners, even after sexual relations, return to their former spouses, he certainly favors the invalidity tradition. However, he also notes that others have a different opinion from his own and that the matter was "sometimes judged otherwise also by some of our predecessors." Shortly after his death, and at the time when the marriage rite was explicitly reckoned as one of the seven principal rites of the church, the teaching of the Latin Church became fixed in favor of the invalidity tradition. Fourth, in the latter part of this century many Roman Catholic theologians have formulated numerous seemingly weighty theological arguments for reinstating the illicity tradition in the West in one or other form.

The *Agreed Statement on the Sanctity of Marriage* also refers to another thorny problem which the commission has

discussed many times:: the ecclesial context required for a
Christian marriage. Since Christian marriage is a sacramental
state within the church it must be sealed in an ecclesial
context. Both churches agree on this. However, the Orthodox
Church following a very old tradition maintains more commonly that the necessary ecclesial context must include the
presence of a priest or bishop who has the intention of acting
as minister of the sacrament. The Roman Catholic Church
requires the presence of a Catholic priest (or deacon) when
this is possible or advisable. But it understands that the ordained minister is an official witness of the church. The partners are traditionally viewed as the ministers of the sacrament.
Hence, the Roman Catholic Church recognizes that Catholics
may enter into a sacramental marriage in the absence of an
ordained minister of the Catholic Church in exceptional cases,
i.e., by reason of a dispensation from the requirement of an
official witness or the unavailability of a major cleric over a
long period of time.

In the effort to overcome these opposing positions, the
commission undertook a historical study of the theology and
practice of marriage in the undivided church. This showed
that the Orthodox theology of the minister of marriage is only
relatively ancient. In the first millennium marriages of Christians before a civil magistrate, for example, were recognized as
Christian marriages in the East and West. Moreover even now,
in practice, the Orthodox recognize marriages between Roman
Catholics as Christian marriages despite the intention of the
priest to act only as an official witness. Also in several places
Orthodox Churches allow, under certain conditions, marriages
between Orthodox and Roman Catholics to take place in a
Roman Catholic Church (Patriarchate of Moscow; Polish Orthodox Church).

On the basis of this study the agreed statement affirms
that "various possibilities of realization of the ecclesial context
are possible as history has shown and no one form of this

realization can be considered to be absolutely normative in all circumstances." Hence, the commission is of the opinion that a reconsideration of the Orthodox theology of the minister of marriage is needed. But it also agrees that the Roman Catholic theology of the minister of marriage should be critically evaluated for it is not altogether clear, and this is the opinion of many Roman Catholic theologians, in what sense the partners can be called the ministers of the sacrament.

Apart from this conclusion, the commission concedes the positive value of both approaches which underscore the necessity of an ecclesial context for Christian marriage. The Orthodox theology does this by insisting on the presence of the ordained minister who, as an essential element of the structure of church, provides a fuller ecclesial setting. Catholic theology emphasizes the ecclesial dimension provided by the presence of two baptized Christians which is an indispensable condition for a truly Christian marriage in both traditions. Where two partners share Christian faith and baptism an ecclesial context obtains which is considered sufficient for sealing a Christian marriage when the more complete context, including the presence of a major cleric, cannot be realized.

The investigation of the theology of the minister of marriage came about because of a more pastoral problem: How should marriage rites involving Orthodox and Roman Catholics be conducted? The commission's opinion was given in *An Agreed Statement on Mixed Marriages*. Here it is stated that, for the present, such marriages ought to take place before an Orthodox priest. This advice was based on the fact that the Orthodox have some difficulty in admitting that a Catholic priest has sufficient intention to fulfill his role. He considers himself to be an official witness of the church; the Orthodox understand the priest to be the minister of the sacrament.

However since the publication of the agreed statement some questions have been raised on the Catholic side. Hence the conclusion to *An Agreed Statement on the Sanctity of*

Marriage notes that the "liturgical celebration of weddings between Orthodox and Roman Catholic partners" needs further study.

It is certainly easier for the Roman Catholic Church to agree to an Orthodox Church wedding since in its tradition the intention of the Orthodox priest to act as minister does not affect the validity of the sacrament. He is considered to act as official witness whether or not he recognizes this. And the partners are understood to be ministers of the sacrament even if they are not aware of it. However, other pastoral concerns raise the question whether the Catholic pastor should, in all cases, acquiesce to an Orthodox Church wedding. For example, the tradition of holding the wedding in the church of the bride may be so important in a particular situation that the Catholic priest might consider it pastorally prudent to advise the couple to decide for a Catholic Church wedding.

There is no doubt that this problem needs more attention. Some general consensus between the Orthodox and Roman Catholic Churches is required to solve the question which the Orthodox still pose about the validity of marriages between Orthodox and Roman Catholics before a Catholic priest. The Orthodox practice of requiring an Orthodox marital ceremony after a marriage between an Orthodox and Roman Catholic in a Roman Catholic ceremony in order to insure validity does not, in fact, resolve the problem from the Orthodox side. Since the Roman Catholic partner considers that he or she has already participated in the sacramental rite of marriage, the Orthodox ceremony is not understood by the Catholic as the celebration of the sacrament of marriage. The intention of the Catholic partner, therefore, calls into question the validity of the Orthodox rite even from the side of the Orthodox.

An Agreed Statement on Mixed Marriages also discussed the role of the Orthodox and Roman Catholic pastors. Both pastors are urged to accept the responsibility for instructing both partners concerning the peculiar difficulties of this marital situation. They are reminded that they should encourage both partners to assume their individual responsibility for the religious upbringing of their children and their duty to respect the religious convictions of one another as well as to support one another's growth in Christ.

The agreed statement refers the decision about the religious upbringing of the children to the couple. They should make the choice based on a prudent judgment which takes into consideration the whole context of the family life. Both pastors are expected to aid the couple in this decision. This advice is based on the premise that if the couple makes a decision that is truly their own, and which is grounded on the conviction of what is best in their concrete situation, there is reasonable hope that both will cooperate in the religious formation of the children. Moreover, there is less chance that this question will provide a source of disunity in the family.

The possible options of the couple are not discussed in detail. The agreed statement at least provides for the possibility of raising the children in either church. The theological basis for this is said to be "our conviction of a common participation (i.e., Orthodox and Roman Catholic Churches) in the mystery of Christ and his church." The commission takes for granted that both churches' preaching of the Gospel in word and act preserves the essentials of Christian tradition and so assures the children's spiritual and intellectual formation in the basic aspects of Christian faith.

Modern legislation in the Orthodox and Roman Catholic Churches does not coincide with the proposal of the agreed statement. In both churches the canonical conditions for approving such marriages have in view the rights of one partner. The "deficient faith" of the other partner is presumed to negate the equality of responsibility of both partners. No account is taken of the personal faith of the partners vis-à-vis one another.

The commission's position, which has precedent in the

history of the relations between these churches, is linked to the insight that (1) both partners have an inalienable right and responsibility with respect to the religious formation of their children; (2) it cannot be determined a priori which form of religious upbringing would be more fruitful in a particular marital situation.

Further study of the question is needed. The mixed marriage does not fit into the scope of the general marriage legislation of either church. It represents a situation which only partially falls within the purview of either church. Hence, the legislative decisions of both churches taken unilaterally do not correspond to the reality of this concrete marriage. When a family is divided between two Christian communities it is in an anomalous situation with respect to the general law of either church. As a social entity it cannot be dealt with by either church's law which is intended for members who are in full communion. Accordingly, it seems opportune at this time that both churches work together to formulate legislation that corresponds to this unique situation. Such action would be an exercise of the communion of the one church of Christ. Hence, whatever concrete laws are enacted must be justified within the theoretical ecclesiology of both churches. Still, this foreseeable problem does not provide sufficient excuse for neglecting the weighty demands of pastoral ministry to these marriages which fall within the sphere of responsibility of both churches.

An Agreed Statement on the Sanctity of Marriage refers to "pastoral problems" in the area of marriage which need further investigation. These include pastoral care of the divorced and an effective ministry to those experiencing failure in the marital state. At present the commission is undertaking an extensive study of these subjects. Especially in the area of the pastoral care of the divorced, it is admitted that both churches still lack a creative approach.

The commission has not yet taken up in any detail the modern ethical questions related to marriage with the exception of abortion. In *An Agreed Statement on Respect for Life* it deplored the decision of the U.S. Supreme Court which fails to recognize the right to life of each and every unborn child. The brief investigation of the questions of artificial birth control and artificial insemination has shown to the commission that the same variety of approaches are found among Orthodox and Roman Catholic theologians.

Conclusion

The work of this commission has been fruitful, especially for the participants. Solid friendships have been developed and a deeper appreciation of the richness and close proximity of both traditions. Nevertheless, this dialogue has not yet served to stimulate a more widespread one between the two churches at the level of the national episcopal conferences and the local parishes. The leadership provided by the bilateral commission, by its very nature, can only be one of example. Concretely it has demonstrated that Orthodoxy and Roman Catholicism can speak together and come to agreement on important theological and pastoral issues. It is the responsibility of others to recognize the significance of this and take appropriate action.

The need for dialogue at the episcopal and parish levels is obvious. A group of experts cannot alone resolve theological and pastoral problems of common concern. Much less can they overcome the divisions between the churches. This can only be done through all the members of both churches who come together to discuss their mutual problems and experience their unity in Christ.

It is understandable why the dialogue has not been realized at the parish level. The Orthodox and Roman Catholic bishops have not, in general, provided the example and called attention to the urgency of this dialogue. The establishment of the bilateral commission has shown the concern of both jurisdictions to promote unity between the two churches. But more is needed.

The decision taken by the Orthodox and Roman Catholic Churches in 1975 to establish an international Orthodox and Roman Catholic bilateral commission for the purpose of theological dialogue may serve to stimulate more direct contact between the Standing Conference of Canonical Orthodox Bishops and the United States Conference of Catholic Bishops. In the opinion of this writer, the time to take this step has come. The work of the bilateral commission, especially on the subject of marriage, has shown the pressing need of this.

Up to this date, however, only the Greek Orthodox Church has shown any initiative in this regard. When at some future time the history of the Orthodox-Roman Catholic relations in the U.S.A. is written, it will have to include an important article which appeared in the Greek Orthodox archdiocesan newspaper the *Orthodox Observer*, March 1, 1978, and which is included in I Appendix. Under the title "Orthodox and Catholic Council Proposed," Rev. Dr. Nicon D. Patrinacos, Ecumenical Officer for the Greek Orthodox Church in the U.S.A., suggested the establishment of an Orthodox-Roman Catholic National Council to deal with common theological and pastoral problems. He shows in a very convincing way that the time is ripe for such a move. It would be a fitting climax to the creative initiative of the Orthodox and Roman Catholic jurisdictions in the U.S.A. in establishing the first national bilateral commission of the Orthodox and Roman Catholic Churches, if these same jurisdictions were the first to form a National Orthodox-Roman Catholic Council.

3.
The International Orthodox-Roman Catholic Dialogue

The announcement of the establishment of the Inter-Orthodox and Roman Catholic Commissions to prepare for theological dialogue was made in 1975. This represents a milestone in the history of the ecumenical movement in this century. In order to fully appreciate this step it is necessary to set it in the context not only of the history of the Orthodox Church involvement in the ecumenical movement of the modern era but also of the history of the growing consciousness of the unity of the autocephalous Orthodox Churches and their need to express this unity. For it is this latter consciousness that made possible the gathering of all independent Orthodox Churches in 1961 and so the possibility of a common decision about entering into dialogue with Rome on the international level. We must also take account of the influence which the ecumenical movement has had on the Roman Catholic Church in the latter part of this century.

In this chapter, a brief survey of the involvement of the two churches in the 20th century ecumenical movement is followed by a discussion of the significance of the Pan-Orthodox Conference for the realization of the Orthodox dialogues with other Christian churches. The third section outlines the history of the Orthodox-Roman Catholic relations since 1960 which led to the decision of 1975. Finally, the present state of progress of the International Orthodox-Roman Catholic Dialogue is described. Some observations are also offered on the direction it may be expected to take in the first and second phases during the next few years.

1. The Orthodox-Roman Catholic Involvement in the Ecumenical Movement

Among the first church leaders to speak in favor of closer cooperation between Christian churches with a view to promoting a common witness to Christ's love and revelation for mankind was the Patriarch of Constantinople, Joachim III. In his encyclical letter, January 2, 1920, addressed "to all churches of Christ, wherever they may be," he urged the churches to turn to one another. This letter is characteristic of the concern which he had shown from the beginning of the century.

Strictly speaking, however, the ecumenical movement of this era had its immediate origin in the Missionary Congress held at Edinburgh in 1910. Here Protestant and Anglican missionaries gathered to discuss the scandal of the divisions of the church which presented an obstacle to the spread of the Gospel. Later that year Bishop Charles Brent, Anglican missionary bishop, reviewing the findings of the congress for the General Convention of the Protestant Episcopal Church in the U.S.A. held in Cincinnati, spoke of the necessity of the unity of the church and called for a world conference on Faith and Order to examine the real differences between churches.

After the First World War, a congress of Protestant and Anglican Churches was held at Stockholm in 1925 under the theme: Life and Work. As a consequence of this meeting, it was decided that two separate commissions should be established: one concerned with the cooperation of churches in solving various social problems; the other to deal with matters of faith and church order with a view to eventual union of churches. The Faith and Order Commission met at Lausanne in 1927 and at Edinburgh in 1937. As might be expected, given the impetus provided by Patriarch Joachim, the Orthodox Church was involved in this whole movement to some extent from the beginning.

When the two commissions, Life and Work and Faith and Order, combined to form the World Council of Churches and met at Amsterdam in 1948, the Orthodox Church was present. In 1960 it entered into full participation in the World Council of Churches under the influence of Patriarch Athenagoras I.

The Roman Catholic Church remained outside the ecumenical movement until 1949. In this year the Holy Office issued an *Instruction on the Ecumenical Movement*. The main point of this document was to encourage Catholics to become involved in the thrust toward unity of churches. The role of Pope John XXIII in promoting contact with the World Council of Churches is well known. His various speeches on the subject of church unity, beginning in 1959, culminated in the founding of the Secretariat for the Promotion of Christian Unity in June 1960. Within a short time, a Joint Working Group was formed between the SPCU and the WCC. This group decided in 1966 on a Joint Theological Commission to study fundamental issues between the Roman Catholic Church and other churches. Now the Roman Catholic Church has full members on the Faith and Order Commission of the WCC.

These movements within the Orthodox and Roman Catholic Churches also involved direct contact with other churches on the national and international levels. The initiative of the Second Vatican Council and its implementation are well known. Regarding the Orthodox Church, it had a long history of contact with the Anglican Communion since the Reformation and negotiations were intensified in this century. The decision to engage fully in the WCC in 1960 did not, however, mean a decision to engage directly in dialogue with any particular churches of the WCC. However, the possibility of moving in this direction was provided by the decision of the Orthodox Church to hold a Pan-Orthodox Conference.

2. The History of the Pan-Orthodox Conference

In September 1961, under the leadership of Patriarch Athenagoras I, the most representative Orthodox assembly since the 8th century met at Rhodes. This meeting was the first concrete step toward preparing for a synod of all independent Orthodox Churches.

Some signs of interest in a general synod had been shown at the International Orthodox Conference held at Constantinople, May 1923. Again in a letter of December 10, 1925, Patriarch Basilius III spoke of convoking a general synod to be held at Mt. Athos during the season of Pentecost, 1926. On April 27, 1926 the Holy Synod of Constantinople announced a general synod but no date was set. The only result was the Inter-Orthodox Conference at Mt. Athos in June 1930. Patriarch Photios II called for a general synod in 1931 to convene at Pentecost, 1932. This resulted in the Inter-Orthodox Conference of theologians at Athens, November/December 1936.

When the Pan-Orthodox Conference was finally realized, Metropolitan Chrysostomos of Myra represented Patriarch Athenagoras I. He served as chairman and supervised the drafting of proposals for the forthcoming synod to be called "The Great and Holy Council of the Holy Orthodox Church." The themes suggested for the synod were the following: (1) faith and dogma: sources of revelation, Scripture and Tradition; (2) liturgy: role of the laity; (3) fasting regulations: need for change; (4) impediments to marriage: reconsideration of marriage laws; (5) calendar question: uniform date of Easter; (6) economy and strictness in application of law.

Two more Pan-Orthodox Conferences were held at Rhodes in 1963 and 1964; a fourth took place at Chambesy (Geneva, Switzerland) in 1968. At these sessions the original agenda of I Rhodes was entertained. But in July 1971, the Preparatory Commission for the forthcoming synod called for a review of the work of the Pan-Orthodox Conference. For this purpose a Pre-Synodal Pan-Orthodox Conference was held at Chambesy, November 21-28, 1976.

At this meeting it was decided that only those topics proposed by seven churches would be included on the agenda of the synod. As a result, three of the original items were retained: (1) fasting regulations; (2) impediments to marriage (clergy and laity); (3) calendar question. To these were added: (4) canonical problems among Orthodox jurisdictions in countries where Orthodoxy has been recently established; (5) relations with non-Orthodox churches; (6) ranking of autocephalous churches; (7) autocephaly and autonomy; (8) conditions under which autonomy is granted to local churches; (9) ecumenical movement and relations of the Orthodox Church to the World Council of Churches; (10) the Orthodox Church's mission to preach freedom and equality among all peoples.

The new items on the agenda include four that deal with the internal relations between the Orthodox Churches; two concerning the relations with other Christian churches and one which treats of the church's mission to the world. The one which interests us the most is no. 5. For the Pan-Orthodox Conference commits the Orthodox Church to think through its relationships to the Roman Catholic Church, as well as to other Christian churches.

During the course of this century the Orthodox Church has been extremely hesitant about engaging in direct theological dialogue with other churches, apart from the Anglican Communion. This was shown at I-II Rhodes. At III Rhodes the decision was taken for "informal dialogue" with other churches. Since that time the Byzantine Orthodox Church has held four unofficial conversations with the Oriental Churches (1964, 1967, 1970, 1971).The Ecumenical Patriarch has met with the Evangelical Church of Germany (1969, 1971, 1973); the Moscow patriarchate with the same churches in 1970, 1972, 1974. The Moscow patriarchate has also held meets with the Roman Catholic Church in 1967, 1970, 1973, 1975. There exists—the International Anglican-Orthodox Joint Doctrinal Commission. In the U.S.A. the Standing Conference has commissions meeting with representatives of the Lutheran and Reformed Churches, as well as the Roman Catholic Church. The last named was discussed in the previous chapter.

3. The Orthodox-Roman Catholic Relations since 1960

Since 1960 slow but steady progress has been made in improving Roman Catholic-Orthodox relations on the international level. The initial overture of real significance was made by Rome. The Orthodox Church was invited to send representatives to the Second Vatican Council which convened October 11, 1962. Nine of the Orthodox Churches voted against official participation. Still the Moscow patriarchate sent unofficial representatives and Patriarch Athenagoras was personally represented by Fr. Schira, a Romanian. Commenting on this refusal of the Orthodox Church to send official representatives, Yves Congar observed that it had missed an important opportunity. This may be so. But it seems clear that the Orthodox Church was simply not ready for such a decision. More preparation was needed before the Orthodox world, as a whole, could accept such a move.

The task of creating the proper climate for serious dialogue between the two churches fell on the shoulders of Patriarch Athenagoras I and Pope Paul VI. Both accepted the responsibility. At the end of the Second Session of Vatican

Council II, December 4, 1963, Pope Paul VI announced his intention to meet with Patriarch Athenagoras I in Jerusalem. The meeting took place during January 1964. Later that year in the *Decree on Ecumenism*, issued on November 21, 1964, the Second Vatican Council extended an invitation to the Orthodox Church to begin a dialogue.

This decree had a very positive effect on the Orthodox Church since it included a formal recognition of the ecclesial status of this church and also spoke of the intimate relation of the two churches in the matter of faith, worship and apostolic ministry. It was followed in the next year by a most significant gesture. On December 7, 1965 both Pope Paul VI and Patriarch Athenagoras I lifted the Anathemas of 1054 simultaneously in Rome and Constantinople. Subsequently Pope Paul visited Istanbul in 1967 and the Patriarch returned the visit during the same year by traveling to Rome.

These gestures proved extremely fruitful. At the Fourth Pan-Orthodox Conference in 1968 an important decision was taken which went beyond III Rhodes. Noting the progress that had been made in relations with Rome, it was agreed that (1) dialogue be encouraged on the level of local churches; (2) local churches be asked to prepare for dialogue with the Roman Catholic Church; (3) special Inter-Orthodox Theological Commissions be organized for dialogue with other churches including the Roman Catholic Church.

The next most important step toward improving relations between the Orthodox and Roman Catholic Churches took place in 1971. Pope Paul VI and Patriarch Athenagoras I exchanged a series of letters about a "common sacramental cup" to which both aspired. This public manifestation of the desire of both church leaders to communicate together in the Eucharist led to an unofficial colloquy between representatives of both churches. It was held at Vienna, April 1-7, 1974. The chairmen were Metropolitan Damaskinos of Tranoupolis, Secretary General of the Preparatory Commission of the Pan-

Orthodox Council, and P. P. Duprey, Undersecretary of the Secretariat for the Promotion of Christian Unity.

The encouraging results of this meeting and further negotiations led to the next major decision. On December 14, 1975, in the Vatican Sistine Chapel, Metropolitan Meliton announced the formation of a special Inter-Orthodox Theological Commission to prepare for formal theological dialogue with Rome, in accord with a Pan-Orthodox decision. The Vatican responded by setting up its own commission.

The church historians and theologians should not have been surprised by the ecumenical outreach of the Orthodox Church in this century. As history shows, the more deeply a church is conscious of its unity, the more profoundly it experiences its catholicity: its inner drive to diffuse itself through the whole world in order to draw the world into itself.

The theologian explains why this consciousness of unity strives to express itself in a catholic outreach. The experience of unity derives from the Spirit by which the church tends always to a deeper unity in Christ. The experience of unity in Christ necessarily entails an experience of the catholicity of the church and so moves the church to strive for greater universality: to draw all humanity into the unity of the Spirit of Christ.

The history of the Orthodox Church in this century shows that the more the Orthodox Church became conscious of its unity: of the unity of the autocephalous churches which constitute it, despite the many internal problems which have surfaced and which seem, at times, capable of rupturing this unity, the more it has become conscious of its catholicity.

From the viewpoint of the historian and theologian it could also be anticipated that this movement outward would eventually focus on the Roman Catholic Church. For these churches formed an undivided church in the first millennium and have preserved the essentials of their ancient doctrines and practices.

But again, from the standpoint of the historian, this

movement of the Orthodox Church toward the Roman Catholic Church could be expected to come only after a great deal of soul-searching and struggle to overcome the deep-seated antipathy caused by numerous unfortunate incidents of the past in which the Latin Church acted as catalyst. The Orthodox still vividly remember who directly caused the reciprocal Anathemas of 1054, who replaced the Patriarch of Constantinople in 1204 and who attempted to rupture national Orthodox Churches by negotiating unity with receptive local churches.

On the other hand, it could be predicted that when the Roman Catholic Church took its major step toward involvement in the ecumenical movement at the Second Vatican Council, it would place great emphasis on contact with the Orthodox Church. This happened. And it comes as no surprise that since that time the Orthodox have changed their ecumenical orientation. Now they give priority to the dialogue with Rome.

4. The Present State of the International Orthodox-Roman Catholic Dialogue

In the long run, the possibility of a fruitful International Orthodox-Roman Catholic Dialogue will depend on a number of conditions. The Orthodox must succeed in holding the Great and Holy Council which will provide the forum for resolving internal problems. It must succeed in creating a Standing Pan-Orthodox Synod with the Ecumenical Patriarch as the honorary primate of the Orthodox Church. Thus it must reach harmonious agreement over the four items on the agenda which deal with the internal relations between the various national churches. Only so will it be able to present a more unified body in its dialogue with Rome: the indispensable condition for the possibility of reaching common agreement with Rome on difficult issues which at present hinder reunion.

The Great and Holy Council must also take a positive attitude toward dialogue with Rome when it considers the fifth item of the proposed agenda. It is precisely here that the work of the international Inter-Orthodox and Roman Catholic commissions, which will be engaged in dialogue, can make a difference.

The role of the international bilateral commission in resolving doctrinal issues which stand in the way of reunion cannot be overestimated. Its findings will provide a concrete basis for the Orthodox Church's judgment concerning the extent to which it is prepared to recognize the Roman Catholic Church as a "sister church" and pursue the work of the reunion.

The Orthodox Church has at hand the Second Vatican Council's statement about the Roman Catholic Church's understanding of its relation to the Orthodox Church. In the *Decree on Ecumenism* it is stated that the Orthodox Church is a church "joined in closest intimacy with us" (no. 15). This has been emphasized by Paul VI. For example, he wrote to the Ecumenical Patriarch in February 1970 that "between our churches and the venerable Orthodox Church there already exists an almost complete, though not yet perfect unity, the result of our common participation in the mystery of Christ and his church." Still the Orthodox Church has not yet made an official statement about its understanding of the ecclesial status of the Roman Catholic Church and its relation to the Orthodox Church. This is understandable since the Orthodox Church has not yet been able to meet together in a council which could resolve this question.

The work of the preparatory commissions for the international dialogue began in October 1976 when the Roman committee met to draw up its suggestions for the agenda. The Orthodox counterpart held its meeting for the same purpose in

June 1977. This was followed by the convening of the Joint Coordinating Group, March 29 to April 1, 1978. On the basis of the reports of the preparatory commissions this group drew up a plan for the official dialogue. It made recommendations concerning the method to be followed and the themes to be considered. While these recommendations remain confidential, we know from published sources what will be the main focus of the discussions in the first stage of this dialogue.

On November 30, 1977 a Catholic delegation visited Phanar, the section of Constantinople where the patriarchate is located. On that occasion Cardinal Willebrands spoke of the progress of the preparation for the International dialogue and Patriarch Demetrios I, who had succeeded the late Athenagoras I in 1972, responded. The exchange is found in II Appendix together with the message read by Metropolitan Meliton, representing the Patriarch, and Pope Paul VI's reply, given on December 7, 1977 at Rome, in which the latter referred to the same subject.

Cardinal Willebrands began by noting that the recent mutual exchanges between Rome and Constantinople are signs of a communion already existing. He based this communion on the common belief in the "sacramental reality of the church," i.e., its mystery dimension: its life in Christ through the Spirit. Still, he said, these churches do not communicate fully on the level of ecclesiastical life and so are hindered from proclaiming their profound union.

To overcome the separation he argues that dialogue should begin with the sacraments. From this source the church is "progressively transformed and developed." Hence it is here that the profound life of the church is found. The rethinking of the sacramental reality of the church, by reflection on the sacramental celebrations, should make possible the clarification of "all the points which are still a source of difficulty" between the two churches. It is here that the churches will discover and recognize one another and find grounds for reconciling the variations in the visible life of both.

Patriarch Demetrios I, in turn, remarked with approval that the Inter-Orthodox Commission had chosen the doctrine of the sacraments as the first and principal subject for the first phase of the dialogue. He went on to say that this offers a favorable field for dialogue since both churches have the same sacraments and agree on the principal doctrinal issues concerning them. Beginning with this common deposit of faith, and not with themes which divide the churches, a constructive dialogue is made possible.

A week later at Rome, in his response to Metropolitan Meliton, Pope Paul VI concurred with Demetrios I: ". . . the dialogue between our churches, based on the sacramental reality itself, benefits from a solid foundation which holds out the hope of overcoming the difficulties which do not yet permit a concelebration of the Eucharist."

We can expect that the dialogue will begin with the one sacrament of God: Christ, as expressed in the sacrament of the church and most fully in the Eucharist of the church. In all likelihood the Eucharist will become the focal point of the initial phase of the dialogue. This will serve as point of departure for a consideration of baptism; mutual recognition of sacraments of the two churches; the relation between sacraments and the canonical structures of the church; the work of the Holy Spirit in the structure and realization of the life of the church.

By beginning with the mystery of the church: the presence of Christ and the Spirit, as proclaimed in the sacramental celebrations, it will be possible to come to a better appreciation not only of the basis of the unity of the church but also of the source of actual unity of Christians among themselves: unity of faith, love and hope generated by Christ in the Spirit. This enables a clearer distinction to be formulated between these basic aspects of the unity of the church and the structural, canonical expressions of this unity.

We can confidently forecast that the fundamental structure of church will be discussed in connection with the theme of the Eucharist. Both churches agree that the church manifests and realizes itself in this celebration. Therefore the local church, which celebrates the Eucharist, is church. However, the extent to which the local church realizes itself as church is measured by its outreach to other churches and not simply by its celebration of the Eucharist.

Both churches are in accord on the following points regarding the local nature of church:

1. The local community around the bishop and other ordained ministers is truly church.

2. The unity of the local church is manifested in Christ and realized most perfectly in the Eucharist.

3. The catholicity of the local church, its outreach to other local churches, measures the extent to which its eucharistic celebration is a realization of church. And this means:

4. The local church is not less church because it is not in communion with other local churches but because it refuses to seek communion with other churches: to exercise a ministry of unity, through its bishop, by fostering, preserving and deepening its communion with other local churches.

Within this general perspective it may be expected that two types of ecclesiology will be judged negatively: a form of Orthodox eucharistic ecclesiology and a form of papal ecclesiology.

There exists in certain Orthodox circles a eucharistic ecclesiology which simply defines church as autonomous, independent local churches consisting of bishop, other ordained ministers and people. This church is seen as a perfect realization of the body of Christ when it celebrates the Eucharist. The fact that it can celebrate the Eucharist shows that all churches are absolutely equal. Therefore no church, or its bishop, can be said to have primacy in teaching and jurisdiction over other churches and their bishops.

There has also existed in Catholic theology a papal eccle-siology which gives disproportionate weight to the role of the pope in the ministerial structure of the church. In this theol-ogy, the church is seen as a world-wide organization in which the local churches are defined as parts of the one reality and so subordinated to the totality which alone has the fullness of the reality of church. Hence, the local bishops are understood as delegates of the one bishop of Rome without rights and duties directly derived from episcopal ordination in the church.

Both views are incorrect. The extreme form of Eucharis-tic ecclesiology exaggerates the autonomy and independence of the local church and so the local bishop. It is not championed by the majority of Orthodox theologians. Still it must be admitted that this theory has highlighted the sacramental nature of the church and episcopal office. It does this by pointing out what the church is through an appeal to the highest form of realization of the church: the communal sacra-mental celebration of eucharistic faith. Thus the church is clearly seen not to be in the first instance a juridically struc-tured social reality but a sacramental social reality. Moreover from this standpoint episcopal office in the church, which has the role of leadership of the eucharistic celebration, is shown to be sacramentally grounded: as having authority and respon-sibility for the local church by divine right.

However, by its very nature the church exists and realizes itself outside the event of common worship where it celebrates its unity in Jesus Christ and consequently the sacramentally based episcopal office is exercised in non-liturgical ways. As the ancient and modern rites of episcopal consecration of the East and West affirm, the bishop is ordained to a pastoral office which includes the threefold function of liturgical lead-ership, teaching and governing. By divine right, the bishop has authority and responsibility for sustaining and promoting the faith in Jesus Christ in his local church by leading worship, teaching and governing. But since this faith is the faith of the whole church, he must listen to what the whole church says about this faith through the medium of the college of bishops. And as a member of the college of bishops he has likewise the authority and responsibility to contribute to the upbuilding of the faith of the whole church.

This sacramental view of the church and episcopal office was espoused by the Second Vatican Council which taught that the local church is truly church and that its bishop has authority by divine right and through episcopal consecration over the local church. It also stated many times that the church most perfectly manifests and realizes itself in the celebration of the Eucharist where the bishop or his representative presides. Finally it affirmed that the college of bishops has authority and responsibility for the world-wide communion of local churches. As a consequence the somewhat totalitarian concept of authority in the church which perdured for several centuries in the West and gained even greater popularity since Vatican Council One can no longer be sustained in theory.

Within this sacramental understanding of the church, as communion of local churches living from Christ in the Spirit and governed by bishops who have authority by divine right, the important question of the primacy of the pope will naturally be discussed in the international dialogue. The papal primacy of teaching and jurisdiction cannot be based on the episcopal ordination of the pope. The pope is a bishop like all other bishops in virtue of episcopal ordination. Also, this primacy cannot be grounded on a distinction between the jurisdictional and sacramental realities of the life of the church. It will be the task of the Roman Catholic commission to show how the Petrine office can be integrated into the church in such a way that its sacramental basis is affirmed and the relative independence of other bishops and their churches is preserved. Obviously this means that the pope will have to be seen first as bishop of Rome and so in the context of a concrete local church. Then it must be shown how in this capacity he has the primacy of service in behalf of the unity and freedom of the church.

No doubt the international dialogue will ultimately focus on the question of the interdependence of local churches on one another and so on the primacy of ministry within the church. These questions which naturally attract the attention of church officials are important. Their solution will advance the movement toward reunion. But when and if an agreement can be reached in this matter there will still remain a number of pastoral problems in need of resolution.

In the second phase of the dialogue, the problem of the education of the members of both churches in each other's tradition will have to be considered. If the goal of the dialogue is eucharistic communion, the membership of both churches will have to come to the realization that they are one in Christ despite their differences in styles of life, liturgy, etc. Instruction will be required. The ways to accomplish this must be a central concern of the international commission.

A second important issue which will certainly surface in the discussions of the commission is the future of the Eastern Catholic Churches which are already in full communion with Rome. In the event of full communion between the Roman Catholic and Orthodox Churches what will be the status of these Eastern Catholic Churches which originated from the missionary work of Constantinople? Should they be directly linked with the Patriarchate of the West, with some patriarchate of the East or exist as independent patriarchates?

The Second Vatican Council did not shed much light on this question. In two separate documents it presented contrasting views of the status of the Orthodox Church and the Eastern Catholic Churches. In the *Decree on Eastern Catholic Churches*, no 25, the Orthodox Church is invited to join itself to the unity of the Catholic Church. In the *Decree on Ecumenism*, no. 14, the Orthodox Church is called a "sister church."

Does Rome's tendency to consider the Eastern Catholics as a "bridge church" show here? How can Eastern Catholics be a bridge church and the Orthodox Church be called a "sister church"?

A third important concern of the later phase of the commission's discussions must be the different practices of the Orthodox and Roman Catholic Churches regarding divorce and remarriage. To what extent can the two different, if not contradictory positions on the question of remarriage after a consummated sacramental marriage exist in an undivided church?

Certainly full communion between the Orthodox and Roman Catholic Churches will render this question relative in the minds of the faithful of both churches if it is not resolved. In effect, if the Roman Catholic Church agrees that the practice of the Orthodox is no hindrance to reunion it will be admitting that the Roman practice merely pertains to church discipline. Therefore this question looms as a serious obstacle to reunion.

The task assigned to the international theological commission is not an easy one. But we may hope that the Spirit of truth will provide both churches with the insight and courage to seek the truth, admit shortcomings and joyfully accept the unity given in Christ through the Spirit and so live together visibly as the one church of Christ.

4.

Roman Catholic Response to Some Theological Concerns of Orthodoxy

At the present time when Roman Catholic and Orthodox theologians are beginning to speak with one another and employ similar theological methods, a number of longstanding disputes are being reconsidered. A number of theological differences which were once considered irreconcilable are now viewed in a new light. There still remain some incompatible theological positions which must be resolved before reunion of the churches is possible. But even here, in many cases, there seems hope for a breakthrough.

Among the issues which no longer seem unresolvable are the different approaches to problems related to the Trinity: (1) knowledge of God; (2) mission of the Spirit to the church; (3) procession of the Spirit within the Trinity. Theological difficulties which still offer a serious challenge to both churches relate more to the area of ecclesiology. Among these are: (1) the identification and interpretation of the significance of the general councils of the whole church; (2) the Petrine office. In this chapter we discuss the progress being made in the rethinking of these topics within Roman Catholic Theology.

1. Knowledge of God

Christian tradition employs two ways of approaching the knowledge of God. The first method begins with the notion of the complete transcendence of God. Since God is wholly other, the grounds of creation, he is best known by a process of eliminating all images and symbols. In this way the mystic gradually ascends to the state of the prayer of quiet and experiences God in the darkness of contemplation. This is the *via negativa* or the apophatic way taught by Eastern and Western spiritual writers.

On the other hand, the scientific theology of the West focuses on the knowledge of God gained through creation. God can be reached through creatures because he manifests himself in creation and salvation history. Christ, in fact, is God's real icon. In him God is present in a positive way. This is the *via affirmativa* or kataphatic way.

Authentic Eastern and Western mysticism always includes apophatic and kataphatic elements. The apophatic way must have a kataphatic basis: above all the icon of God, Jesus Christ and the liturgy of the church. The kataphatic way in both traditions is not the end of the journey toward God in this life. It should lead to the apophatic. The approved spiritual writers of both churches speak of a superior knowledge of God which is not mediated merely through the recalling of the humanity of Jesus Christ. Rather he is the door to a higher contemplation as is the liturgy of the church. One must pass through this door, though it must not be set aside or forgotten.

The knowledge attained through the kataphatic way is imperfect. This is the teaching of the West. The Fourth Lateran Council, 1215, states that between the creator and creation no similarity can be expressed without including a greater dissimilarity. Scholastic theology adds that when one attributed the perfections of creatures to God, it should be noted that these perfections are only analogously found in

God. They exist in God in a superior way and without the limitations of created perfections.

This theology also speaks of a more perfect knowledge of God derived from mystical prayer. But this more direct experience of God is also understood to be mediated through creation. The totally new way of knowing God granted to the just in heaven is explained through the concept of the *lumen gloriae*. This light through which the just enjoy the beatific vision is, however, also a created supernatural gift. By it the just see God, though not in a comprehensive way. God remains incomprehensible even in the beatific vision.

The Orthodox Church's speculation on the knowledge of God takes a different path, dominated by the speculation of Gregory of Palamas (d. 1359). He speaks of a superior knowledge of God granted within the apophatic way. While the creature can never know God comprehensively, a new way of knowing God is caused by a light radiating from God himself: an uncreated light, divine but distinguished from the divine essence.

From the standpoint of scholastic theology this theory is untenable. It contradicts the teaching about the infinity of God. To attribute a real distinction in God other than that of the opposition of relations of Persons to one another is to predicate a superior and inferior deity in the mystery of God. Gregory, however, precisely denies that the divine energies constitute a distinct person. They are personalized insofar as derived from the Trinity of Persons in the Godhead. Through these energies the divine life which belongs to the Persons of the Trinity is granted to human beings. They are rooted in the divine essence. But it is only because God is personal that his existence is not limited to his essence.

For Gregory the ontological existence of personhood is revealed by the self-emptying toward others. The divine energies represent God's existence: his outpouring love outside his essence in creation. They are the manifestation that God is

personal in relation to us. Through them God is revealed
outside himself as existence toward others (= personal). But
at the same time they manifest that the internal life of God is
personal. For God cannot be for us what he is not in himself.

Recently Roman Catholic theology has taken a more
positive and sympathetic approach to Gregory's basic concern.
It is more commonly recognized that behind the symbolic
language he is affirming the reality of God's personal communion with mankind in the body of Christ made possible by the
communication of the life proper to God and, at the same
time, God's absolute transcendence.

It is not likely that the different approaches to the knowledge and nature of God of the East and West will constitute a
serious theological difficulty for the future. Neither view can
be completely situated at the level of statements of faith.
Rather they represent developments which from divergent
perspectives make valuable contributions to the theological
enterprise.

2. Mission of the Spirit
   to the Church

In the medieval period, scholastic theology's speculation
on the unity of the divine nature led to the conclusion that all
operations outside the Trinity are indistinctly common to the
Father, Son and Spirit. Consequently the mission of the Spirit
to the church was interpreted in terms of mere "appropri-
ation" because of the aptness of predicating sanctificaton of
the Spirit. Thus the ancient traditional teaching of the personal mission of the Spirit was volatilized. The Orthodox, on
the other hand, continued to begin their theologizing from the
Persons in the Trinity not the divine nature. Hence they
maintained the teaching about the personal mission of the
Spirit to the church.

These divergent approaches to the theology of the Spirit are no longer a cause of dispute. Already in the 19th century M. J. Scheeben popularized the teaching about the personal mission of the Spirit to the church to some degree in the West. More recently H. Muhlen, a German theologian, has led Catholic theology further along the same line. Generally speaking, this theology now takes more seriously the personal mission of the Spirit to the church and this has led to a rethinking of the theology of the church. The church is now seen more clearly as a continuation of the mission of the Spirit to Christ rather than simply as a continuation of the incarnation. The implications of this new view still have not been sufficiently developed.

3. The Procession of the Spirit within the Trinity

The Niceno-Constantinopolitan Creed is not a draft of a profession of faith drawn up by a general council of the church. It derives from a formulation of the faith used in Jerusalem in the middle of the fourth century. Within the next century it gained in popularity in the East. After the Council of Chalcedon approved it in 451, it became widely used in both the East and West.

In this symbol of faith originally the Spirit is said to proceed from the Father. However, already in Spanish territories, at the latest in the sixth century, we read: ". . . proceeds from the Father and the Son (*filioque*)." This insertion of the *filioque* corresponds to the Western view of the relation of the Spirit to the Son already discussed in Augustine. By the ninth century the *filioque* was quite commonly used in Gaul. Pope Leo III (d. 816) disapproved the custom for disciplinary reasons. But the Greeks, since Patriarch Photius (869), claimed it to be heretical. However, the insertion was made in the creed used in Rome in 1014 without consulting the Greeks. Since that time this gesture has been the cause of numerous disputes.

Currently, Roman Catholic scholars are more inclined to agree with the Orthodox that the decision of Rome failed to respect the mutual understanding of East and West that no additions be made to the creed without consulting the whole church. Moreover, Roman Catholic theology is more open to the opinion that its inclusion is not required. The *filioque* teaching seems to be more generally accepted as not only a legitimate but perhaps the best way of thinking about the procession of the Spirit. Still many Catholic theologians will argue that it is a theological theory which has no place in a creed intended to express the common faith of the East and West.

4. Ecumenical Councils

In recent Roman Catholic ecclesiology two questions have been raised concerning ecumenical councils. The first concerns the qualification of general councils held in the West after the schism and approved by the pope. The second relates to the question of the subsequent recognition and reception of the decrees of general councils by the whole church.

Some Roman Catholic theologians, including Vatican officials, point out that no list of ecumenical councils exists which has been imposed with dogmatic authority. Rome lists general councils held in the West under the title "ecumenical." But the attribution is not a dogmatic statement. It reflects popular usage. Pope Paul VI reflects how Catholic theology is willing to consider the notion of varying degrees of councils approved by a pope. In an official public letter of October 5, 1974 addressed to Cardinal Willebrands on the occasion of the eighth centenary of the Second Council of Lyons, 1274, he wrote: "This council of Lyons counted as the sixth of the general synods held in the West. . . ."

This distinction is important. It opens the way to the removal of an obstacle to reunion with the Orthodox. In the event of reunion it is unlikely that the Orthodox would be asked to affirm those councils of the West, held after the schism, as ecumenical. Therefore *per se* they would not be bound to affirm the conciliar decisions as having binding force on them, but only insofar as they proclaim the faith of the undivided church.

Modern Roman Catholic theology has, in several instances, warned against an overly mechanistic understanding of general councils and the value of their decrees. A case is being made for some sort of subsequent reception by the whole church. It is taken for granted that councils are guided by the Spirit who inspires pastors to address doctrinal and pastoral problems. But it is understood that councils usually address very limited issues and in troubled times and so may not focus on the center of revelation. Hence the conclusion is reached that conciliar decrees must be read in the light of Scripture, liturgy and authentic Christian practice which express the faith more fully. These decrees should not be considered so absolute as to eliminate all responsibility for reinterpreting the faith for new situations.

This approach seems to be in harmony with the insight of Orthodoxy which speaks of the necessity of the subsequent reception of conciliar decrees by the whole church in order that they may be known as statements of the faith. Perhaps further dialogue will provide grounds for a common statement about the function of the whole church in the subsequent reception of the teaching of a general council of the church.

5. The Petrine Office

The most difficult problem in the theological discussion between Orthodox and Roman Catholic theologians centers around the role of the pope in the universal church.

The Orthodox Church recognizes a certain primacy in the church which is interpreted in several ways. Currently it is more generally understood as a primacy of honor and awarded to the Patriarch of Constantinople. While all bishops are considered equal in episcopal dignity, there are firsts among equals in the local churches. As first bishop the Patriarch of Constantinople is spokesman for Orthodoxy and exercises leadership in general councils. But he does not exercise primacy of jurisdiction and teaching authority over the other patriarchates.

The Roman Catholic Church attributes to the pope primacy of jurisdiction and teaching authority over the whole church. It is opposed to the Orthodox view of primacy of honor. In recent years, however, a new discussion has begun over the office of Peter. It promises to produce results which will open the way to serious dialogue with the Orthodox Church. The direction of this discussion can be summarized in four steps.

(1) In the New Testament writings a number of images are associated with Peter. He is missionary fisherman, shepherd of the flock, model martyr, recipient of a special revelation, confessor of the true faith, overseer of doctrine and church discipline. These images seem to grow out of one another as developments in the life of the church call for a new model of church leadership. Thus Peter the Christian fisherman (missionary) becomes the shepherd, the model of the leader of the local community, when settled churches begin to develop.

The awareness that the experience of the life of the church caused a shift in thinking about Peter, which nevertheless displays a certain consistency, prompts biblical exegetes to ask a new question about the relation of Peter to the bishop of Rome. The former question: Did Jesus install Peter as the first pope? is changed to: To what extent does the later use of the image of Peter in relation to the papacy correspond to the trajectory of the New Testament?

(2) A response to this question depends on discovering the grounds for the appeal made by Roman bishops to Matthew 16:17-19 as support for their authoritative role in the whole church.

Initially the exercise of this role was not caused by the common acceptance of a theological theory of the primacy of Peter and succession on the office of Peter based on the exegesis of a word of Jesus. Rather sporadically in the third and consistently from the fourth century Matthew 16:17-19 served as supplementary support to legitimize a leadership role and claim which developed on the grounds of a variety of historical themes and considerations. The fact that Rome was the capital city of the empire comes immediately to mind. But perhaps of greater importance was the experience of the exceptional fidelity of the Roman community in time of persecution and the purity of its doctrine. To this must be added the persuasion that Peter and Paul were martyred in Rome and the motif of passage from Jerusalem to Rome which the whole church read in the *Acts of the Apostles.*

A reasonable explanation of the historical data must place the experience of the life of the church in the foreground. The general awareness of Rome's preeminence in supporting the faith of the whole church led to a re-reading of the New Testament. Peter's role was being fulfilled by the Roman Church and it was accepted by Rome as its permanent task. Consequently, the theological grounding of the office of Peter, not unlike the process of development of the images of Peter in the New Testament, was Scripture appropriated in the context of the lived faith of the church.

(3) The process by which Scripture was re-read in the light of the experience of the faith of the church in the patristic period resulted in awarding the office of Peter to the Roman

bishops has its counterpart in the 20th century. It is instructive to analyze how the Second Vatican Council received the teaching of the First Vatican Council concerning the primacy of the pope.

The First Vatican Council defined that the pope has primacy of jurisdiction and teaching authority in the church. This teaching was accepted by the Second Vatican Council but with an interpretation. Whereas the First Vatican Council stressed the primacy of the pope, this council explicitly situated it within the context of episcopal collegiality. In fact it accepted the view of the minority at Vatican I which argued for a more thorough discussion of the relationship of the primacy of the pope to the college of bishops.

(4) The foregoing considerations lead to the conclusion that there is an office of Peter given once for all and which cannot be arbitrarily manipulated. At the same time, the history of this office shows that it has been reinterpreted in the light of Scripture, Tradition and newer knowledge and experience of the life of faith of the church. Consequently, it cannot be said a priori that the present understanding of the Office of Peter and the style in which it is exercised will never change. Present crises and newer experiences could conceivably give rise to a new interpretation and concrete form of this office.

Already there are indications of a new development in the understanding of the office of Peter which, if accepted, will involve a new style of the ministry of this office. This new thinking derives from a reconsideration of the basic task which Scripture and Tradition award to this office: service in behalf of the unity of the church.

One of the roles assigned to the office of Peter in the service of the unity of the church is the supervision of the daily life of the whole church. At Vatican Council I this task was described as a primacy of jurisdiction and in practice this jurisdiction was given the widest meaning. It involved immediate overseeing of the minutiae of the life of each local church.

The Second Vatican Council, on the other hand, called attention to the role of the college of bishops in the service of the unity of the church and emphasized the divine right of each bishop to govern his own church. However, the Second Vatican Council did not resolve the question of the relationship of pope to bishops in the matter of jurisdiction. Rather by extending the sharing of the bishops in the actual jurisdiction of the pope, it left the church with the question: To what extent should the pope share jurisdiction with the bishops?

During the last ten years, however, a more basic question is being raised frequently by Catholic theologians. They are asking: What is the theological meaning of jurisdiction? A rereading of Scripture provides the answer that the spiritual authority in the church should exercise a service of the Gospel of freedom. Since the office of Peter has this authority in a preeminent way it should exercise a pastoral primacy which is specially characterized by its effectiveness in liberating Christians for Christian freedom. The pope should be the model pastor who protects Christian freedom. As center of unity and communication he must be the one who safeguards the unity of faith but in all other things promotes variety and freedom to meet the particular needs of local churches.

This understanding of the pastoral primacy corresponds to the Second Vatican Council's teaching about the relationship of pope and bishops to the church. The pope is both member of the church and at the same time stands vis-à-vis the church as representative of Christ, the one head. The bishops are also both members of the church and by reason of their ordination have authority from Christ and so represent him in their local churches. Thus the church appears as a communion of local churches which are each church in the full sense if they witness to the communion which they have in Jesus Christ by communicating with one another.

During the first millennium when the concept of the church as a communion of local churches was alive in both the

East and West, the pope fitted into a communion structure in which local bishops exercised more complete jurisdictional authority. This communion ecclesiology disappeared in theory and practice in the West during the second millennium. The reform of the church at the beginning of the second millennium under Pope Gregory VII led to the freedom of the church from state. But it also resulted in the dissolution of the old church communion and a centralistic understanding of the unity of the church as the local churches looked to Rome for protection from the state.

Nowadays the West is returning to the ancient communion ecclesiology. The local churches are considered as churches in the full sense and not as "parts of the universal church." So the pope is not viewed as a super-bishop who delegates jurisdiction to local bishops. But the problem remains as to how the pope should fit into this concept of church. How can this communion ecclesiology be put into practice? A synthesis of the developments of the two millennia seems to provide an answer. The pope should exercise a ministry in behalf of the freedom of the local churches and at the same time do so within the context of the communion of local churches.

Several suggestions have been made as to how this synthesis might be concretely realized. Prescinding from minor differences they can be reduced to two. There is the opinion that the pope should be exclusively a servant of the unity of the universal church. As a super-bishop or, rather, president of the local churches he would communicate with the local churches through synods, commissions, etc. This opinion must be disregarded. It separates jurisdiction from the sacramental life of the church and so would secularize the papacy.

Only the way of the old church remains. The pope should be understood primarily as bishop of the local church of Rome. This view implies a loss of administrative responsibility. But it has the advantage of allowing the peculiarity of the

Petrine office to shine forth. It would allow for a qualitative concentration on the essentials of the Petrine service of the unity of the church: strengthening the brethren in the one faith in Jesus Christ. Since it entails more freedom for the local churches to accommodate to their concrete situations, it would manifest that only in the one faith is unity necessary and that in all else variety and freedom should reign.

The service of the pope in behalf of the unity of the church must be above all a service of the faith of the church. For the unity of the church is primarily and above all a unity in the one faith in the one God, the Father of the one Lord Jesus Christ. Hence when the First Vatican Council defined the primacy of the pope it did so by stressing his teaching authority. This definition calls for further comment since it offers a major difficulty for the Orthodox Church.

The First Vatican Council defined that the pope possesses that infallibility which Jesus Christ gave to his church when he speaks *ex cathedra*, i.e., when he definitively decides, as shepherd and teacher of all Christians with the highest apostolic authority, that a teaching about faith or morals is to be held by the whole church. The Second Vatican Council, on the other hand, speaks of the infallibility of the church as such and as a whole. It affirms that the totality of believers in communion with the teaching office of the church cannot err: "This characteristic is shown in the supernatural appreciation of the faith of the whole people, when, from the bishops to the least of the faithful, they manifest a universal consent in matters of faith and morals" (*Constitution on the Church*, no. 12). How then is the infallibility of the pope related to the infallibility of the church?

The infallibility of the pope presupposes the infallibility of the church. For it is only meaningful if the church infallibly believes this infallibility. On the other hand, the church, as a human society, can only speak and act through those who represent it. In order to be capable of actualizing the infallibility of the whole church there is need for the infallibility of the pope.

But the pope should not be understood as functioning merely to express the current majority opinion of the church. Rather he represents the unity of the church through history since he represents Jesus Christ. He can take a stand against the leading opinions of the day since he represents the sovereignty of the Gospel over the church. This is expressed in the formula of the First Vatican Council which states that definitions of the pope made *ex cathedra* are "irreformable from himself (*ex sese*), not from the consent of the church." This statement means that such definitions ultimately bind the church and so are not subject to a higher juridical authority. It does not exclude that the pope must listen to the witness of the church beforehand or that his definition needs the subsequent interpretative reception of the church. Rather it affirms that the Gospel stands over the church.

The position of the Roman Catholic Church is this: The infallibility of the pope and that of the church form a structural whole. The infallibility of the pope refers to the question of how the church can speak in an irreformable way; how it can speak in a way which ultimately binds the faithful. The infallibility of the church vis-à-vis the pope refers to the capability of the church to ultimately bind itself to his witness to the Gospel. Hence, to avoid ambiguity which the word *infallibility* occasions it is better to speak of a capability of ultimately binding the community and of the community ultimately binding itself.

This infallibility cannot be reduced to indefectibility. Hans Küng has argued that human statements are false or true after they are concretely situated. The church needs, according to him, binding formulas of faith in extreme situations where a decisive yes or no is demanded. But such statements can only be pragmatic formulas conditioned by the context. In another context they can be erroneous. Thus he prefers to speak of the indefectibility of the church. It will not be destroyed but preserved in the truth in spite of the ever threatening possibility of error in matters of faith and morals.

The reduction of the infallibility of the church to indestructibility was rejected by the Vatican Instruction *Mysterium ecclesiae* in 1973. It is also opposed by the majority of Catholic theologians. For the claim to ultimate binding can only be grounded on a claim to truth. Unconditional truth alone corresponds to unconditional binding. But here precisely a more basic question is raised which lies behind the concepts of ecclesial and papal infallibility. What is the relationship between unconditional divine truth and historically conditioned human expressions of truth?

The response of Catholic theology must begin with the understanding of the church as place of the permanent presence of the Word of God and so sacrament of the truth. As sacrament of the truth the church cannot depart from the truth of Jesus Christ. But the church is only sacrament of the truth, sign which points to the proper content of the faith. Hence, church dogmas are not the proper content and goal of the faith. God who has revealed himself in Jesus Christ in the Spirit is the proper content and goal of the faith. Dogmas are symbols, introductions into the mystery of the faith. The dissimilarity of each of their expressions is greater than the similarity with the thing signified. Therefore dogmas must be understood as historically open questions. They are always open to a new interpretation.

Moreover, dogmas are not the ultimate grounds of the faith. The ultimate ground of faith is not the authoritative witness of the church but rather, as First Vatican Council teaches, the authority of God revealing himself. Hence, only insofar as one is convinced in the faith, i.e., in the Spirit, of the truth of an offical statement can he and ought he to accept it. Therefore there exists in all ecclesial mediation a more fundamental immediacy of the Christian to God. It is this immedi-

acy which constitutes the ultimate basis of the claim of infallibility. It is God who ultimately binds the believing conscience
to the witness of faith.

Since it is in one's conscience that the ultimate binding to
the witness of faith given by the pope takes place, this demands of the ecclesiastical authority a less authoritative and
more argumentative style of teaching the faith. A teaching is
required which corresponds more to the service of the unity of
the faith in Christian freedom.

Summary and Conclusion

This view of the office of Peter dispenses with the overly
juridical and authoritative style of exercise of authority. It
concentrates on the essentials of this office: its role in fostering
the life of faith in which Christian freedom reigns. It calls for a
style of ministry in which the spiritual and sacramental service
of the office is given greater visibility. It underlines the need
for a charismatic teacher who can witness to the Word of God
in such a way that the Christian conscience is able to accept it
in Christian freedom.

The Orthodox understanding of the primacy corresponds
in good measure to this interpretation of the office of Peter.
The extent to which they are able to accept it, however,
remains problematic. For they are faced with the decision to
accept the position that the primacy of the whole church was
decided once for all, and by the experience of the faith of the
ancient church, to accrue to the Roman Church. This will
surely offer a most serious difficulty for the Orthodox Church
in its dialogue with Rome. It will also offer a challenge to the
Roman Catholic partners of the dialogue. Why should the
primacy of the whole church be always allotted to the Roman
Church? This question will have to be answered in a very
convincing way before reunion of the churches is possible.

If this question is resolved to the satisfaction of the Orthodox and Roman Catholic Churches, and if the Orthodox Church can agree to the concept of a pastoral primacy in the service of the unity of the church, as outlined above, the Petrine office should no longer present a major obstacle to reunion. A brief comparison of the contemporary Orthodox and Roman Catholic theologies of the primacy within the church, which also serves to summarize the previous discussion of the office of Peter, shows this to be true.

The Orthodox view the church as a communion of local churches which finds its prototype in the Trinity where there is distinction of Persons but unity based on eternal love. In keeping with this view the bishops, sharing in the ministry of Christ, are equal among themselves as far as episcopal dignity is concerned. They and their churches are bound together by love not external law. The source of this love in the church is the Spirit who grounds the whole structure of the church.

Since the local churches are in communion with one another, interdependent on one another, the local bishops are organized in such a way that common action and cooperation are possible. Therefore, there are firsts among equals in the local churches and a first among equals within the whole body of the bishops of the universal church.

However, the Orthodox Church views the church structure of the Roman Catholic Church as unsatisfactory because the first among equals of the bishops exercises an exaggerated form of jurisdiction and teaching authority. As a result he is no longer considered equal in dignity with other bishops but rather over them. He has become in Roman Catholic theology, and in practice, a super-bishop of the whole church.

From the recent discussions of the office of Peter among Roman Catholic theologians, and the teaching of the Second Vatican Council to some extent, it is clear that the monarchical model of hierarchy of bishops is out of favor. The unitarian view: one God—one Kingdom—one King, which had been transferred to the church: one God—one Church—one pope, is discarded for the Trinitarian model: unity in multiplicity and unity through mutual penetration of one by the other.

The Trinitarian logic grounds the unity of the church in the multiplicity of churches which are bound together through communion of faith, worship and government (brotherly service). In this view the church and the office of Peter are realities formed historically in the power of the Spirit, which can only be understood in the Spirit and must be continually realized anew in the Spirit.

Since the Spirit is given to the church and to each member of the church, the church is a communion of persons. The basic structure of the church is a brotherhood in the Spirit. This Spirit is likewise the Spirit of Jesus Christ. Bestowed once for all through Jesus Christ, the Spirit has a completely Christ-ward reference. The Spirit always refers the church to Christ, its head. This position of Christ vis-à-vis the church is represented authoritatively by ecclesiastical office, and in a comprehensive way by the office of Peter. Thereby office is bound to the measure of Jesus Christ. It can exercise authority in the church of Jesus Christ only in the way it was exercised by Jesus Christ: the way of self-emptying, renunciation of force, privation and powerlessness. It must validate the liberating power of the Gospel of love of Jesus Christ. Only in such a following of Jesus Christ does ecclesiastical authority lead the church in the Spirit on the way to the Father.

A conception of the office of Peter as service in the unity and freedom of the church could become a synthesis of the historical developments of the first and second millennia. It could help to reconcile the Catholic principle of authority and the modern principle of freedom. It could offer a way to greater ecumenical unity of the church and, in particular, of the Roman Catholic and Orthodox Churches.

The rethinking of the office of Peter in the International

dialogue between the Orthodox and Roman Catholic Churches could become a time of grace for the whole church of Christ. This will happen in the measure that both sides are open to interpreting it from the essence of Christianity: the following of Christ in the Spirit to the glory of the Father.

5.
Appendix:
U.S.A. and Related Documents

1. An Agreed Statement on the Holy Eucharist.

We, the members of the Orthodox-Catholic Consultation, have met and discussed our understanding of the Holy Eucharist. After a dialogue, based on separately prepared papers, we affirm our remarkable and fundamental agreement on the following:

1. The Holy Eucharist is the memorial of the history of salvation, especially the life, death, resurrection, and glorification of Jesus Christ.

2. In this eucharistic meal, according to the promise of Christ, the Father sends the Spirit to consecrate the elements to be the body and blood of Jesus Christ and to sanctify the faithful.

3. The eucharistic sacrifice involves the active presence of Christ, the High Priest, acting through the Christian community, drawing it into his saving worship. Through celebration of the Eucharist the redemptive blessings are bestowed on the living and the dead for whom intercession is made.

4. Through the eating of the eucharistic body and drinking of the eucharistic blood, the faithful, who through Baptism became adopted sons of the Father, are nourished as the one body of Christ, and are built up as temples of the Holy Spirit.

5. In the eucharistic celebration we not only commend

ourselves and each other and all our lives unto Christ, but at the same time accept the mandate of service of the Gospel of Jesus Christ to mediate salvation to the world.

6. Through the Eucharist the believer is transformed into the glory of the Lord and in this the transfiguration of the whole cosmos is anticipated. Therefore the faithful have the mission to witness to this transforming activity of the Spirit.

Recognizing the importance of this consensus, we are aware that serious differences exist in our understanding of the church, eucharistic discipline, and pastoral practice which now prevent us from communicating in one another's churches. Our task should consist in exploring further how these differences are related to the agreement stated above and how they can be resolved.

Worcester, Massachusetts
December 13, 1969
(Fifth meeting)

2. An Agreed Statement on Mixed Marriages

The recent dialogue between the Orthodox and Catholic Churches has led to a deeper appreciation of their common tradition of faith. This exploration has helped us to reassess some specific theological and pastoral problems in the area of Christian marriage. We recognize the practical difficulties which couples continue to face when they enter a mixed marriage as long as their churches are divided on matters of doctrine and styles of Christian life. Because of these difficulties both of our churches discourage mixed marriages

I. Pastoral Problems

1. We recognize that under the conditions of modern life these mixed marriages will continue to take place. For this

reason counseling of couples entering such unions by pastors of both churches is imperative. In this counseling the sincerely held religious convictions of each party, based upon their church's tradition, must be respected, especially as regards the nature of marriage and the style of life in marriage.

2. One area in which counseling by the pastors is desirable concerns the Christian upbringing of the children. We recognize the responsibility of each partner to raise their children in the faith of their respective churches. We encourage the pastors of both churches to counsel these couples in the hope of helping to resolve the problem which this responsibility creates. Specific decisions should be made by the couple only after informed and serious deliberation. Whether the decision is made to raise the children in the Orthodox or Catholic tradition, both partners should take an active role in the Christian upbringing of the children and in establishing their marriage as a stable Christian union. The basis for this pastoral counsel is not religious indifferentism, but our conviction of a common participation in the mystery of Christ and his Church.

3. Each partner should be reminded of the obligation to respect the religious convictions and practice of the other and mutually to support and encourage the other in growing into the fullness of the Christian life.

II. Theological Problems

1. According to the view of the Orthodox Church the marriage of an Orthodox can only be performed by an Orthodox priest as the minister of the sacrament. In the view of the Catholic Church the contracting partners are the ministers of the sacrament, and the required presence of a Catholic major cleric as witness of the Church can be dispensed with for weighty reasons. In view of this, we recommend that the Catholic Church, as a normative practice, allow the Catholic

party of a proposed marriage with an Orthodox to be married with the Orthodox priest officiating. This procedure should, however, take place only after consultation by the partners with both pastors.

2. We plan the further study of the Orthodox and Catholic traditional teaching concerning marriage.

New York City
May 20, 1970
(Sixth meeting)

3. An Agreed Statement on Respect for Life

We, the members of the Orthodox-Roman Catholic Bilateral Consultation in the United States, after extensive discussions on the sanctity of marriage, feel compelled to make a statement concerning the inviolability of human life in all its forms.

We recognize that human life is a gift of God entrusted to mankind and so feel the necessity of expressing our shared conviction about its sacred character in concrete and active ways. It is true that the Christian community's concern has recently seemed to be selective and disproportionate in this regard, e.g., in the anti-abortion campaign. Too often human life has been threatened or even destroyed, especially during times of war, internal strife, and violence, with little or no protestation from the Christian leadership. Unfortunately, the impression has frequently been given that churchmen are more concerned with establishing the legitimacy of war or capital punishment than with the preservation of human life. We know that this has been a scandal for many, both believers and unbelievers.

We feel constrained at this point in history to affirm that the "right to life" implies a right to a decent life and to full human development, not merely to a marginal existence.

We affirm that the furthering of this goal for the unborn, the mentally retarded, the aging, and the underprivileged is our duty on a global as well as a domestic scale.

We deplore in particular the U.S. Supreme Court's decision failing to recognize the rights of the unborn—a decision which has led to widespread indiscriminate early abortion.

We affirm our common Christian tradition with regard to the right of the unborn to life.

We acknowledge our responsibility to mediate the love of Christ, especially to the troubled expectant mother, and thus make possible the transmission and nurturing of new life and its fully human development.

We urge our churches and all believers to take a concrete stand on this matter at this time and to exemplify this evangelical imperative in their personal lives and professional decisions.

Washington, D.C.
May 24, 1974
(10th meeting)

4. An Agreed Statement on the Church

Issued by the Orthodox-Roman Catholic Bilateral Consultation in the U.S.A.

1. Christianity is distinguished by its faith in the Blessed Trinity. In the light of this revelation Christianity must interpret the world and every aspect of it. This revelation has obvious implications for the interpretation of the nature of the church.

2. The church is the communion of believers living in Jesus Christ and the Spirit with the Father. It has its origin and prototype in the Trinity in which there is both distinction of persons and unity based on love, not subordination.

3. Since the church in history is constituted by the Spirit

as the body of Christ, the continuity of the church with its origin results from the active presence of the Spirit. This continuity is expressed in and by historical forms (such as Scripture and sacraments) which give visibility to the continuing presence of the Spirit but it does not result merely from a historical process.

4. Sharing in Christ and the Spirit, the local church is at once independent in its corporate existence: a church, and at the same time interdependent in relation to other churches.

The independent existence of the local church is expressed best in its eucharistic celebration. The sacramental celebration of the Lord's presence in the midst of his people through the working of the Spirit both proclaims the most profound realization of the church and realizes what it proclaims in the measure that the community opens itself to the Spirit.

5. The independence of local eucharistic communities, in the disciplinary and constitutional spheres, was curtailed in the early church as soon as priests became leaders of the local churches. The dependence of local churches on the territorial bishop found its counterpart in the dependence of bishops on the "first" bishop (archbishop, metropolitan, patriarch) as territories were divided among bishops.

The interplay of independence and communality on the local, territorial, and patriarchal levels mirrors the church's prototype: the Trinity, which the church can only approach.

6. The fundamental equality of all local churches is based on their historical and pneumatological continuity with the church of the apostles. However, a real hierarchy of churches was recognized in response to the demands of the mission of the church. Still this did not and cannot exclude the fundamental equality of all churches.

7. The Catholic and Orthodox Churches explain differently the meaning of this hierarchy of churches.

The Catholic Church recognizes that the position of Peter in the college of the apostles finds visible expression in the Bishop of Rome who exercises those prerogatives defined by Vatican Council I within the whole church of Christ in virtue of this primacy.

The Orthodox Church finds this teaching at variance with its understanding of primacy within the whole church. It appears to destroy the tension between independence and collegiality. For interdependence, a basic condition for collegiality, appears to be removed as a consequence of the jurisdictional and teaching role attributed to the Patriarch of the West by Vatican Council I. The Orthodox believe that a necessary primacy in the church depends on the consent of the church and is at present exercised by the Patriarch of Constantinople.

8. Our two traditions are not easily harmonized. Yet we believe that the Spirit is ever active to show us the way by which we can live together as one and many. We have the hope that we will be open to his promptings wherever they may lead. "For only so will harmony reign, in order that God through the Lord in the Holy Spirit may be glorified, the Father and the Son and the Holy Spirit" (Apostolic Canons, Cn. 34).

New York City
December 10, 1974
(11th meeting)

5. The Pastoral Office: A Joint Statement

Introduction

1. Both the Orthodox and the Roman Catholic Churches acknowledge that the pastoral office, exercised by bishops and

priests, is an essential element of the structure of the church founded by Jesus Christ.

The members of this dialogue, while recognizing this fact, also understand that certain changes have taken place in the exercise and in the understanding of this office both in the early church and later in the separated churches.

2. In the interest of furthering the mutual recognition of the pastoral office exercised in each of our churches this Consultation has judged it useful:

(a) To record the results of its discussions of the understanding and function of pastoral office in the history of the Orthodox and the Roman Catholic Churches;

(b) To formulate a statement concerning important elements of our common understanding of pastoral office;

(c) To single out recent discussions on the subject of pastoral office which seem to require the serious attention of both churches.

I. Historical Considerations

According to the New Testament, the witnesses to the resurrection formed the original church on the basis of their common faith in Christ. Within this group, chosen witnesses were given special authority by the risen Lord to exercise pastoral leadership. While this leadership seems to have been exercised in a variety of concrete ways in the New Testament period, the tendency towards a presbyteral form of government, presided over by a bishop, was apparently more common.

At the outset of the second century this movement towards a more monoepiscopal form of local church government continues to develop. In the course of the second and third centuries the bishop gradually emerges everywhere as the center of unity of his own local church and the visible point of contact with other local churches. He is responsible for faith and order locally.

During this period the presbyterate comes to share in the exercise of more aspects of the pastoral office in subordination to the bishop. This subordinate role is seen especially in presbyteral ordination, which is reserved to bishops.

In accord with the development whereby the presbyterate is explicitly included in the pastoral office of the bishop under virtually all aspects, the presbyter is viewed as having the same relationship to Christ as the bishop. Both are seen directly to represent Christ before the community and, at the same time, to represent the church, as confessing believers, in their official acts.

However, the tendency in the West towards the dissociation of pastoral office from its ecclesial context provided a difference of perspective on the conditions for the valid exercise of the functions of pastoral office. Thus, while Orthodoxy never accepted in principle the concept of "absolute ordination," this notion did find acceptance in the West in the late Middle Ages.

However, the Second Vatican Council's stress on the pastoral dimension of priestly office corrected the weakness of western theology of priesthood. Furthermore, the fathers of the council refocused attention on two major traditional themes: (a) the sacramental nature of episcopal consecration; and (b) the collegial or corporate character of each of these orders, a theme which harmonizes with the traditional Orthodox perspective.

II. Our Common Understanding of the Pastoral Office in the Orthodox and Catholic Traditions

Although the historical perspective points out many divergent practices through the centuries, the members of the Consultation recognize the following as important elements towards the development of a consensus.

1. In the rites of ordination of bishop and presbyter a commission is bestowed by the Holy Spirit to build up the church (Eph. 4:12) on the cornerstone of Christ and the foundation of the apostles (Eph. 2:20).

2. Presiding at the Eucharist belongs to those ordained to pastoral office: bishops and presbyters. This exclusive connection between ordination to the pastoral office and the celebration of the Eucharist affirms that the pastoral office is realized most directly in this celebration of the faith. In the Eucharist the Lord builds up his church by uniting it with his saving worship and communicating his personal presence through his sacramental body and blood (I Cor. 10:16-17).

3. The offices of bishop and presbyter are different realizations of the sacrament of order. The different rites for ordination of bishop and presbyter show that a sacramental conferral of office takes place by the laying on of hands with the ordination prayer which expresses the particular significance of each office.

4. While both bishop and presbyter share the one ministry of Christ, the bishop exercises authoritative leadership over the whole community. The presbyter shares in the pastoral office under the bishop.

5. Ordination in apostolic succession is required for the bestowal of pastoral office because pastoral office is an essential element of the sacramental reality of the church: Ordination effectively proclaims that pastoral office is founded on Christ and the Spirit who give the grace to accomplish the task of exercising the ministry of the apostles.

6. The fundamental reason why pastoral office is required for the celebration of the Eucharist lies in the relationship of pastoral office to church and the relationship of Eucha-

rist to church. Pastoral office is a constitutive element of the structure of church and the Eucharist is the place where the church most perfectly expresses and realizes itself. Consequently, the requirement of correspondence between the comprehensive ecclesial reality and the Eucharist dictates the exercise of pastoral office.

7. Bishops and presbyters can only represent Christ as bishops and presbyters when they exercise the pastoral office of the church. Therefore, the church can recognize only an ordination which involves a bishop with a pastoral office and a candidate with a concrete title of service.

8. We have a common understanding of these effects of sacramental ordination: (a) the ordained is claimed permanently for the service of the church and so cannot be reordained; (b) in the exercise of his office, he is distinct but not separated from the community; (c) he is not dependent merely on his subjective capabilities for the exercise of his service, since he receives the special bestowal of the Spirit in ordination.

Catholic theologians have explained these elements in terms of *character*, priestly *character*. Similar elements are included in Orthodox understanding of priesthood as a *charisma*. Both character and charisma stress the relationship of the ordained to the gift of the Holy Spirit on which the exercise of his ministry in service to the community depends.

III. Recent Trends and Disputed Questions in Both Traditions

Roman Catholic and Orthodox theologians today have addressed themselves to several major topics related to the theology of pastoral office.

1. Some Roman Catholic theologians are challenging the traditional presentation of the pastoral office as direct repre-

sentation of Christ. They interpret pastoral office as directly representing the faith of the church and consequently, Christ who is the living source of the faith. From this viewpoint the peculiarity of pastoral office is situated in the public guardianship of the common matter of all believers: the mission of Christ.

2. The traditional exclusion of women from ordination to the pastoral office affects both Catholic and Orthodox theologians, but in a differing way. Concerning this issue, Catholic theologians are examining biblical data, traditional practice, theological and anthropological data. Since they have not reached a consensus, the question remains disputed among them.

Some Catholic theologians share the position of those Orthodox theologians who reaffirm the traditional practice of excluding women from the pastoral office and base this on the necessity of the iconic representation of Christ in the person of bishops and presbyters.

3. Two of the issues touching the life-style of those called to pastoral office come under serious consideration in both traditions: (a) the compatibility of ordination with occupations which are not directly part of the pastoral office, and (b) the existing practice of celibacy.

(a) Both Catholic and Orthodox theologians see a long tradition of ordained persons exercising certain occupations compatible with the pastoral office which are also seen to serve the sanctification of society.

(b) In the Orthodox Church questions are raised concerning a married episcopate and marriage after ordination. Among Catholics of the Latin rite the celibacy issue focuses on the possibility of also committing the pastoral office to a married clergy.

4. Faced with the important issue of mutual recognition of ministries, both Orthodox and Roman Catholic theologians are searching for criteria leading to such a goal.

Conclusion

The members of the Consultation draw the following conclusions: despite differing emphases, both churches agree on the nature and forms of pastoral office; theologians of both traditions perceive that they have common as well as distinct questions to be resolved.

Washington, D.C.
May 19, 1976
(14th meeting)

6. The Principle of Economy: A Joint Statement

1. Members of the Orthodox-Roman Catholic Bilateral Consultation in the United States, having met since 1965, have examined openly, in a spirit of Christian faith and fraternal charity, a wide spectrum of theological questions judged to be crucial for mutual understanding between our two churches.

2. One topic which has been discussed with particular interest, especially during 1975 and 1976, has been *oikonomia* or ecclesiastical "economy." Because of the possible relevance of economy to the question of mutual recognition of churches, this topic, which has been important for the Orthodox, has received increasing attention among Anglicans and Roman Catholics in recent years.

3. In its discussion of economy the Consultation considered an introductory report prepared in 1971 by the Inter-Orthodox Preparatory Commission for the forthcoming Great Council of the Orthodox Church. Some Orthodox and Roman Catholic members were dissatisfied with the interpretation it gave to certain texts and historical incidents but found it a useful beginning for further discussion.

4. Our investigation has shown:

(a) The wealth of meanings which economy has had over the centuries;

(b) Some weaknesses in recent presentations of economy;

(c) The significance of economy for our ongoing ecumenical discussion.

5. At the most basic level, the Greek word *oikonomia* means management, arrangement, or determination in the strictly literal sense. A few overtones add to this basic meaning. *Oikonomia* may imply accommodation, prudent adaptation of means to an end, diplomacy and strategy and even dissimulation and the "pious lie." But *oikonomia* can also have highly positive connotations. It suggests the idea of stewardship, of management on behalf of another, on behalf of a superior.

6. In the New Testament the word *oikonomia* occurs nine times: Luke 16:2, 3, 4; 1 Corinthians 9:17; Ephesians 1:10, 3:2; 3:9; Colossians 1:25, and 1 Timothy 1:4. In the Parable of the Steward, Luke 16, the word refers generically to stewardship, house management. In other New Testament usages such as Ephesians 3:9, the word is used to refer to God's purpose or *prothesis*, the economy of the mystery hidden for ages in God who created all things.

Also in Ephesians 1:8-10 we read that God "has made known to us in all wisdom and insight the mystery of his will, according to his purpose which he set forth in Christ as a plan for the fullness of time (*oikonomian tou pleromatos ton kairon*) to unite all things in him, things in heaven and things on earth." This usage is closely related to the patristic idea that in and through his person the incarnate and risen Christ brings to fulfillment all of creation (*anakephalaiosis*). The Pauline corpus of letters uses *oikonomia* to refer to Paul's own ministry or pastoral office to make the word of God fully known.

7. These New Testament usages of *oikonomia* are further expanded by the fathers' understanding as summarized by the Interorthodox Preparatory Commission's report which states:

"Apart from the meaning which concerns us here, the term *oikonomia* also denotes the divine purpose of *prothesis* (Eph. 1:10, 3:9-11), the mode of existence of the one Godhead in Trinity through mutual indwelling (*perichoresis*), its broad action in the world through the church, divine providence, the savior's incarnation, the whole redeeming work of our Lord Jesus Christ and all the operations through which human nature was made manifest in the Son, from the time of his incarnation to his ascension into heaven."

God is seen as arranging all for the purpose of man's salvation and eternal well-being; and man fashioned in the image and likeness of God is viewed as being called to imitate this divine activity.

8. The word *oikonomia* later acquired additional uses in ecclesiastical contexts, in particular:

(a) The administration of penance, the arranging or managing of a penitent's reconciliation to the church;

(b) The reception of those turning to the church from heresy or schism;

(c) The restoration of repentant clergy and the reception of heretical or schismatic clergy as ordained.

In all these areas, however, the understanding of economy as responsible stewardship, imitating the divine economy, is maintained, excluding arbitrariness or capriciousness.

9. Recent presentations of economy often have included the following elements:

(a) Economy understood as a departure from or suspension of strict application (*akribeia*) of the church's canons and disciplinary norms, in many respects analogous to the West's *dispensatio*.

(b) Economy applied not only to canon law and church discipline, but to the sacraments as well. In this context, it has been argued, for example that all non-Orthodox sacraments, from the point of view of strictness, are null and void but that the Orthodox

Church can, by economy, treat non-Orthodox sacraments as valid. These views imply that the application of economy to the sacraments may vary according to circumstances, including such pastoral considerations as the attitude of the non-Orthodox group toward Orthodoxy, the well-being of the Orthodox flock, and the ultimate salvation of the person or groups that contemplate entering Orthodoxy.

10. These recent interpretations do not, in the judgment of the Consultation, do justice to the genuine whole tradition underlying the concept and practice of economy. The church of Christ is not a legalistic system whereby every prescription has identical importance, especially when ancient canons do not directly address contemporary issues. Nor can the application of economy make something invalid to be valid, or what is valid to be invalid. Because the risen Christ has entrusted to the church a stewardship of prudence and freedom to listen to the promptings of the Holy Spirit about today's problems of church unity, a proper understanding of economy involves the exercise of spiritual discernment.

We hope and pray therefore that our churches can come to discern in each other the same faith, that they can come to recognize each other as sister churches celebrating the same sacraments, and thus enter into full ecclesial communion.

Washington, D.C.
May 19, 1976
(14th meeting)

7. An Agreed Statement on the Sanctity of Marriage

Introduction

At a time when the sacred character of married life is radically threatened by contrary lifestyles, we the members of the Orthodox-Roman Catholic Consultation feel called by the Lord to speak from the depth of our common faith and to affirm the profound meaning, the "glory and honor," of married life in Christ.

I. The Sacramental Character of Marriage

For Christians of both the Orthodox and Roman Catholic Churches marriage is a sacrament. Through the prayers and actions of our wedding rites we profess the presence of Christ in the Spirit and believe that it is the Lord who unites a man and a woman in a life of mutual love. In this sacred union, husband and wife are called by Christ not only to live and work together, but also to share their Christian life so that each with the aid of the other may progress through the Holy Spirit in the life of holiness and so achieve Christian perfection. This relationship between husband and wife is established and sanctified by the Lord. As a sacred vocation, marriage mirrors the union of Christ and the church (Eph. 5:23).

Christ affirmed and blessed the oneness and profound significance of marriage. Christian tradition, following his teaching, has always proclaimed the sanctity of marriage. It has defined marriage as the fundamental relationship in which a man and woman, by total sharing with each other, seek their own growth in holiness and that of their children, and thus show forth the presence on earth of God's kingdom.

II. Enduring Vocation

The special character of the human relationship established through marriage has always been recognized in the Christian tradition. By sanctifying the marital bond, the church affirms a permanent commitment to personal union, which is expressed in the free giving and acceptance of each other by a man and a woman. The sacrament of marriage serves as an admirable example of the union which exists between God and the believer. The Old Testament uses marriage to describe the covenant relationship betwen God and his people (Hosea). The Letter to the Ephesians sees marriage as the type of relationship which exists between Christ and his church (Eph. 5:31-35). Consequently both the Orthodox and Roman Catholic churches affirm the permanent character of Christian marriage: "What God has joined together, let no man put asunder" (Mt. 19:6).

However, the Orthodox Church, out of consideration of the human realities, permits divorces, after it exhausts all possible efforts to save the marriage and tolerates remarriages in order to avoid further human tragedies. The Roman Catholic Church recognizes the dissolution of sacramental non-consummated marriages either through solemn religious profession or by papal dispensation. To resolve the personal and pastoral issues of failed marriages which have been consummated an inquiry is often undertaken to uncover whether there exists some initial defect in the marriage covenant which would render the marriage invalid.

III. The Redeeming Effect of Marital Love

A total sharing of a life of love and concern is not possible apart from God. The limitations of human relationships do not allow for a giving and receiving which fulfill the partners. However, in the life of the church, God gives the possibility of continual progress in the deepening of human relationships. By opening the eyes of faith to the vision that these relationships have as their goal, God offers a more intimate union with himself. Through the liberating effect of divine love, experienced through human love, believers are led away from self-centeredness and self-idolatry. The Gospel indicates the direction that this love must ultimately take: toward intimate union with the One Who alone can satisfy the fundamental yearning of people for self-fulfillment.

Given this vision of reality, Christian tradition recognizes that the total devotion of the married partners implies as its goal a relationship with God. It teaches, moreover, that the love which liberates them to seek union with God and which is the source of sanctification for them is made possible through the presence of the Spirit of God within them.

Through the love manifested in marriage, an important witness is given to the world of the love of God in Christ for all people. The partners in Christian marriage have the task, as witnesses of redemption, to accept as the inner law of their personal relationship that love which determines the relationship between Christ and the church: "Husbands, love your wives as Christ loved the church and gave himself up for her" (Eph.5:25). Through this love which liberates believers from selfish interests and sanctifies their relationships, the Christian husband and wife find the inspiration in turn to minister in loving service to others.

IV. Theological Clarifications on Christian Marriage

In the teaching of the Orthodox and Roman Catholic Churches a sacramental marriage requires both the mutual consent of the believing Christian partners and God's blessing imparted through the ministry of the church.

At present there are differences in the concrete ways in which this ministry must be exercised in order to fulfill the theological and canonical norms for marriage in our two churches. There are also differences in the theological interpretation of this diversity. Thus the Othodox Church accepts as sacramental only those marriages sanctified in the liturgical life of the church by being blessed by an Orthodox priest.

The Catholic Church accepts as sacramental the marriages which are celebrated before a Catholic priest or even a deacon, but it also envisions some exceptional cases in which, by reason of a dispensation or the unavailability of a priest or deacon, Catholics may enter into a sacramental marriage in the absence of an ordained minister of the church.

An examination of the diversities of practice and theology concerning the required ecclesial context for Christian marriage that have existed in both traditions demonstrates that the present differences must be considered to pertain more to the level of secondary theological reflection than to that of dogma. Both churches have always agreed that the ecclesial context is constitutive of the Christian sacrament of marriage. Within this fundamental agreement various possibilities of realization are possible as history has shown and no one form of this realization can be considered to be absolutely normative in all circumstances.

V. Plans for Further Study

The members of the Orthodox-Roman Catholic Consultation give thanks to God for this common faith in the sanctity of marriage which we share in our sister churches. We recognize however that pastoral problems remain to be studied in depth, such as the liturgical celebration of weddings between Orthodox and Roman Catholic partners and the religious upbringing of children in such families. We continue to explore these questions out of a common vision of marriage and with confidence in the guidance of the Holy Spirit.

New York, N.Y.
December 8, 1978
(19th meeting)

8. Reaction of Orthodox-Roman Catholic Dialogue to the Agenda of the Great and Holy Council of the Orthodox Church

Introduction

The agenda for the forthcoming Great and Holy Council of the Orthodox Church was formulated by the Pre-Synodal Pan-Orthodox Conference, in Chambesy, Geneva, November 21-28, 1976. At the recommendation of His Eminence Metropolitan Meliton, chairman of the Conference, and at the invitation of His Eminence Archbishop Iakovos, co-chairman of our Consultation, the Orthodox-Roman Catholic Consultation in the USA discussed this agenda during its meeting in Washington, D.C., September 28-29, 1977. The Consultation welcomed the agenda as an important step toward the future Great and Holy Council of the Orthodox Church. The following suggestions summarize various observations on the agenda by members of the Consultation. We hope that these suggestions may be of some value and of some service in the preparation of the study documents to be used as the basis of the Great Council's initial discussions.

The Agenda

Topics 1-3. The first three topics (fasting regulations, impediments to marriage, calendar) involve practical issues which deserve the attention of the Orthodox Churches. They are a fitting subject of a Great Council both because a common solution to these issues would enhance the daily life of the Orthodox Christians, and because they offer to the Council the opportunity for reflection on religious issues in the context of today's world.

Topic 1. We understand that some changes in fasting practices are advisable in view of the changing conditions and rhythm of life in some geographical areas of the Orthodox Church. It is not altogether clear, because of insufficient study, what has been the result of the changes pertaining to fasting regulations within the Roman Catholic Church. This should provide the basis for the exercise of caution in the matter of proposed changes within the Orthodox Church. Disciplinary changes pertaining to fasting practices do not automatically bring about the hoped for spiritual fruits without careful preaching and instruction about the reasons for these adaptations. Another question to be raised with regard to these changes is to what extent common practices are necessary to preserve the unity of the church. Finally, discussion about fasting practices should, above all, seriously raise the question of the proper Christian attitudes toward the material world, modern consumerism, availability of foods, modern hedonism, ecology, religious discipline in contemporary society, and the like.

Topic 2. The issue regarding impediments to marriage, pertaining to both clergy and laity, as well as the possible issue of the eligibility of married clergy for the episcopate, requires discussion on the basis of an explicitly formulated theology of marriage, the presbyterate, and the episcopate. Other related themes to be dealt with are human sexuality in general, celibacy and monasticism.

Topic 3. With regard to the calendar question, the impact of Christian agreement on a common Easter date would be considerable both within and without the Christian world. The calendar question also offers an opportunity to address the question of the relationship of the church to modern science. However, a caution may also be sounded: unprepared changes in calendar matters could signal enormous pastoral problems.

Topic 4. It seems to us that the resolution of the *Diaspora* problem might serve to better express the communion ecclesiology of the Orthodox Church. The question of the *Diaspora* should be investigated against the background of the idea of the *catholicity* of the church. An attempt in this regard has already been made at the Second World Conference of the Orthodox School of Theology, Penteli, Athens, August 19-29, 1976.

Topic 5. On the question of the relationship of the Orthodox Church to other Christian churches and communities, special attention should be given to promoting closer relations with the Oriental Churches, the Roman Catholic Church, the Old Catholic Church, and the Anglican Communion. We see that this may involve a thorough study of the principles which have traditionally determined Orthodox views regarding the *ecclesial status* of "separated Christians," and "separated churches."

Topic 6. The question of the ranking of autocephalous churches raises the issue of the practical and theological significance of rank *per se* within the Orthodox Churches. Why, for instance, has the actual importance—past or present—of certain churches in fostering the life of the entire church been the crucial factor in their gaining prominence in rank among their family of churches?

Topic 7. It seems to us that under the theme of autonomy and autocephaly some consideration should be given to the *limits of uniformity* compatible with the unity of the church.

Topic 8. We feel that the consideration of the terms under which autonomy is granted to local churches might take in view the history of the Roman Catholic Church's practice of removing the status of "missionary church" from locally established churches. The history of the relationship between Rome and the Roman Catholic Church of North and South America, as well as Africa, may be useful in this matter. In this connection, the Anglican model of granting independence to missionary churches may also be instructive for the Orthodox Church.

Topic 9. We hold that the presence of the Orthodox Church in the World Council of Churches is a valuable witness of the apostolic and catholic tradition. We feel that Orthodox participation in the ecumenical movement as outlined by the Patriarchal Encyclical of 1920 is an indispensable factor in Christian efforts toward cooperation and unity between Christian churches and communities.

Topic 10. We believe that in proclaiming Christian ideals to the world the church may explicitly call attention to what it has learned from its experience in the world concerning basic Christian ideals. Hence theological reflection is needed on the presence of the Holy Spirit in the world outside the church and the values of the world in the eyes of the church. Under this topic the following specific themes may be given special attention:

(a) Justice and human rights;

(b) Ethical Consensus on many important issues such as sexuality, cohabitation without marriage, abortion, medical issues pertaining to the preservation of life, and the like; and

(c) Study of the roles and methods of effective preaching, Christian education, and liturgical celebration toward spiritual renewal, i.e., the nature of the experience of the living God over against contemporary secularism and the modern experience of the "absence of God."

Conclusion

The agenda of the Great and Holy Council of the Orthodox Church has in view the status and unity of the Orthodox Church primarily in practical terms. However, these matters cannot be adequately discussed without raising deeper theological issues about the nature of discipline, unity, the church, the

Gospel, and life. The Great Council can settle the practical isues in order to strengthen the life of the Orthodox Church. It can also make a real contribution to the proclamation of the Gospel in today's world through the witness of an effective Orthodox consensus on important theological issues pertaining to the church's presence in today's world.

Washington, D.C.
September 29, 1977
(16th meeting)

9. A Statement by the Orthodox and Roman Catholic Bilateral Consultation on Persecution of the Greek Orthodox Community in Turkey

Introduction

Since 1965 in the United States, we the "Orthodox and Roman Catholic Bilateral Consultation," an official group of churchmen, university and seminary professors, have been investigating matters of mutual concern between Orthodox and Roman Catholic Churches. The participants in this Consultation have been offically designated by the respective ecclesiastical authorities.

At our most recent Consultation which took place in New York City, January 24-25, 1978, this statement of concern was drafted, in the first place, by the Roman Catholic participants. They propose to submit it to the National Conference of Catholic Bishops of the United States, with the request that the Conference consider it as a matter of grave significance and take appropriate action. The Orthodox participants in the Consultation unanimously concur in the positions taken below. This statement is issued therefore as a formal statement of the Orthodox and Roman Catholic Bilateral Consultation.

A Statement of Concern

In recent months the Turkish government has taken a series of injurious actions against the Greek Orthodox community in Turkey. This Consultation is deeply concerned about this grave situation that violates even the most basic human rights. The history of restrictive measures and outright persecutions by Turkish officials against the Greek Orthodox minority community, reflected in recent years by the closing of the historic Theological School of Halki, is already well known. However, in more recent times, further discriminatory measures have been imposed by Turkish authorities which limit the leaders of the Greek Orthodox community in the exercise of their legitimate religious rights. For example, millions of liras in taxes have been imposed by Turkish authorities upon the schools and churches of the Greek Orthodox community in Istanbul. At the same time, the Turkish government has refused to issue passports and permits for certain hierarchs and many Turkish citizens of Greek descent to travel abroad. By such actions Turkish officials have seriously interfered with the exercise of the worldwide religious responsibilities of the Ecumenical Patriarchate of Constantinople.

These violations of human rights and religious freedom are in themselves reasons for protest. In addition, we, the members of this Consultation wish to underline the historic significance of the Orthodox See of Constantinople in its present geographical situation for witnessing to the continuity of the Christian church. The oppression of the Greek Orthodox in Turkey and the threat to the very existence there of the Ecumenical Patriarchate are all the more serious in this period when the cause of religious unity and world peace has been fostered by the growing relationships between the Ecumenical

Patriarch and all the Orthodox Churches with the late Pope John XXIII, His Holiness Pope Paul VI and with Christians everywhere.

We express our shock and outrage at these actions and we dedicate ourselves in fraternal concern to continued protests against these measures.

New York City
January 25, 1978
(17th meeting)

10. Orthodox and Catholic Council Proposed— Can Become Vehicle of a Theology of Christian Living

For the last decade or so a group of Orthodox and Catholic theologians have met twice a year to examine together certain fundamental issues that keep the two Churches diverse in belief and separate in organization and government. The Consultation is under the joint chairmanship of Archbishop Iakovos and Cardinal Baum. They both believe in the imperative need to bring the two great Churches into the closest possible contact in the face of the many contemporary hostile trends and practices that seriously threaten not only the effectiveness but also the very being of the entire Church as well.

Thus, the work of the Consultation is of paramount importance to all and indeed sacred, attempting—as it does in the measure of its resources—to pull together forces that had succeeded in the past in destructively violating the most obvious foundational Apostolic aphorism of the Christian ecclesia: Christ cannot be divided. As a matter of fact, this Consultation is for now the only ongoing dialogue between Orthodox and Catholics and its findings are received with great interest by theologians, congregations, and the central authorities of the two Churches, in Rome and Constantinople.

Up to about a year ago, the Consultation occupied itself
with differing beliefs and practices that were of the utmost
importance for theologians but of little direct import on the
personal experience of the peoples of either Church. But the
last and current subject of the Consultation, marriage, is of
immediate and vital concern to all who take marital conjuga-
tion seriously as an experience of personal rights and obliga-
tions that no other human association implies or exhibits.

As the work of finding out and stating the differing
positions in theory and practice on marriage progressed, many
members of the Consultation came to realize that a theological
statement of positions and a possible reconciliation between
their respective most fundamental precepts on marriage would
not by any means exhaust the subject; nor would it free them
from the additional and equally sacred obligation of translat-
ing their theology of marriage into patterns of marital experience for our people.

A mere statement of theological positions, unrelated to
the present day immense moral task faced by conscientious
marital partners, would indeed be in line with past ecclesiastical attitudes we now attempt to remedy. Then, pronounce-
ments were made primarily in pursuit of our own institutional
aims but with little or no regard for the human situation
around us. As someone said, however, if theology is what its
name signifies, that is, reasoning about God, this reasoning is
not done for the sake of God but for the sake of humanity.
Thus, a theology that does not relate its aims and findings to
serving the believer becomes an aimless contemplation worth
no more than other such contemplations.

It was realized, then, that to tell our people that the
concept of marriage as a sacrament is practically identical
between the two Churches and to present them with the
virtues of Christian marriage as patterns of personal conduct
to be followed would do little or nothing to help them in terms
of personal acquiescence, or of living in the context of so many

other types of relationships between a man and a woman that have gained a strong footing in today's cultural setting.

Actually, aphorisms of this kind tend to prove either counterproductive or, at best, leave people cold, disappointed and helpless. A lofty theology that looks at people from on high and expects them to climb to its own heights instead of itself descending to the level of their weakness, creates vacuums that sooner or later will be filled by all kinds of humanistic interpretations. Thus, any statement on marriage on the part of a body of this synthesis and hopeful expectations should encompass much more than theological conclusions.

This is the first time in a thousand years that East and West have found a way to speak and listen to each other and then to speak to others with one mind and one voice on matters that surpass argumentations and quarrels about the Church as the instrument of institutional powers. Now, they seem to concern themselves with the Church as the peoples of God whose identity and responsibilities as Christians by far surpass their membership in one particular Church.

The Orthodox-Catholic Consultation could gradually develop into a National Orthodox and Catholic Council in the United States, with wide and effective representation of both Churches and with a scope including but not limited by theological dialogue. Since any separation of true theology from life is unrealistic and unproductive, this Council could become the vehicle of a theology of Christian living far and beyond mere dogmatical tabulations and argumentations, and could also create in the hearts of the peoples of the two Churches the inner sense of facing together the problems and visions of present day intelligent living and of responding together on the strength of their common sacramental life and ecclesial nearness to adversities, attacks, and all kinds of philosophies and lifestyles that violate the dictates of the Christian Gospel.

Beyond that, a Council of this kind could pronounce on

and seek remedies for a number of social and national issues that touch on occasion on the very quality of our peoples' lives and leave them—if unguided and unconvinced—in a state of helplessness and heightened susceptibility to dangerous preachings and practices.

Perhaps few of us fully realize the extent and depth of the feeling of security our peoples would have knowing that their two Churches—possessors of the genuineness of Christian antiquity—live after all the Christian experience together, and when speaking on contemporary problems derive their authority from the wealth and originality of their tradition according to which the soul of humanity has not changed throughout human development, in spite of humanity's advances in recognizing and assuming considerable control over natural and mental realities. Consequently, the Christ-centered essence of human experience remains and will remain the only way out of the difficulties and impasses in which individuals succeed in entrenching themselves on occasion.

Organizationally, the Standing Conference of Canonical Orthodox Bishops in America and the National Conference of Catholic Bishops could supply the authority and determine the level, function, and constitutional perimeter of a body of this kind. Bringing bishops and other clergymen in frequent and informal contact can do much more toward unity than the most successful theological dialogues.

Considering the fact that dogmatical variance and division has been mainly the product of separate reasoning about God and his Church and of living the life of his Church apart from each other, the resulting estrangement and enmity cannot be eliminated but by living the life of the Spirit together just as we partake of the same national and cultural experience in this country and express ourselves via the same linguistic medium and thought patterns. The divine prompting exhibited by both Patriarch Athenagoras and Pope Paul in selecting personal contact in preference to theological talking has established a pattern for all future dialogues.

Returning briefly to the subject of marriage as a striking example of what a Council of the kind sketched above can do, one must realize that the marital bond is extremely complex. It includes, apart from its religious character, a number of other experiences deriving from situations and influences that involve disciplines other than theology, such as, psychology, sociology, ethical theories, politics, etc.

To encounter successfully those trends and practices we consider opposite to the Christian nature of marriage, we should know, understand, and be able to refute the motivations and underlying forces that spearhead these trends and practices. Rejecting them on the strength of our theological positions might be self-evident and sufficient for us, but it is not necessarily so for many other people who are neither theologians nor that sufficiently imbued with the precepts of biblical morality on the subject. Thus, our refutation must be done on their own ground and by people who are experts in the disciplines that supply to these objectionable lifestyles their strength and appeal to the people who have adopted them.

This means that while the theologians will supply the foundation—our theological positions—to the arguments against these objectionable beliefs and practices, the arguments themselves must derive from and be of a dialectical structure that is understood by those who have grown up with an exclusively rational outlook on man and his cosmos. It would be of no profit to us and of no service to our people to require the latter to switch from their everyday rationality and scientific standards to a religious reality they find impossible to support by their daily experience.

Our Consultation will have to enlist the knowledge and talents of experts on the subjects we deliberate—whenever these deal with the peoples' lives—and on the conclusions we intend to set before our congregations as standards of behavior. It is in the reality and ensuing relationships of everyday life that our people want and need guidance. Guidance and protection of this kind, coming from both Churches, would prove influential beyond the membership of our two Churches and would tend to establish norms not easily rejected by anyone. This, unhesitatingly, can be called real service to the people of God.

Editor's note: Fr. Patrinacos is the Ecumenical Officer for the Greek Orthodox Church in the United States and a member of the Orthodox-Catholic Consultation.

Rev. Dr. Nicon D. Patrinacos

6.

Appendix:
Official Statements of the Patriarchate of Constantinople and the Roman Catholic Church Concerning the International Dialogue

1. Delegation of the Catholic Church at the Phanar: November 30, 1977

On the feast of Saint Andrew (30 November), Patron of the Church of Constantinople, a Catholic delegation visited the Phanar in return for the visit of the Ecumenical Patriarchate to Rome on the feast of Saint Peter (cf. *Information Service,* n. 35).

This annual exchange of visits for the celebration of the patrons of the Churches of Rome and Constantinople is an expression of fraternal communion, and offers an occasion for a regular exchange of information with a view to improving co-ordination in the search for full unity.

The Catholic delegation was composed of Cardinal John Willebrands, the president of the Secretariat, Msgr. Charles Moeller, secretary, and Father Duprey, under-secretary.

In addition to participating in the liturgical celebration,

the delegation was received by the Ecumenical Patriarch, and conversations were held with the synodal commission of the Ecumenical Patriarchate for relations with the Catholic Church.

At the conclusion of the eucharistic liturgy of the feast of Saint Andrew, the following addresses were given in the church:

1) *Speech of Cardinal Willebrands*

Your Holiness,

In communion of faith, in union of charity, and animated by a lively hope, we join today in prayer with Your Holiness, with the venerable brothers of the Holy Synod, and with all the clergy and the faithful, in honor of Saint Andrew, protector of this patriarchal and ecumenical see.

Once again, the Lord has given us this great spiritual joy.

The presence, here, of this Catholic delegation sent by His Holiness Pope Paul VI, as also the presence in Rome for the feast of the Apostles Peter and Paul of the delegation sent there by Your Holiness, is a sign of the mutual fraternal ties which, year by year, become closer and more demanding for our two Churches. These are signs of ecclesial communion.

These last few years, the Spirit of Truth has led us to become aware that this communion is founded on the common patrimony which comes to us from Holy Scripture, a patrimony that was lived and transmitted through the Tradition of the Church, illuminated through the reflection of the Fathers, defended and proclaimed in seven Councils which we, Catholics and Orthodox alike, consider to be ecumenical, and which were all held in these regions that are renowned among Christians everywhere.

Is it not the sacramental reality which makes this communion solid and substantially unalterable? We believe, in effect, Catholics and Orthodox, that the Church is the great sacrament of salvation, the pillar and foundation of truth. This profound conviction is the fundamental reality on which the relations between our two Churches, the relations between sister Churches, are based.

In the course of its journey through history, the Church has encountered and undergone many difficulties, both interior and exterior. Among these, the ones from which it has suffered most are the divergences and divisions which have torn the seamless robe of Christ. In patience and charity it is trying to overcome these through the power of the Spirit given to it by the risen Christ. It needs to overcome them in order to be able to proclaim its own mystery to the world. It is in it and through it that the Kingdom of God is built up. The Spirit, the definitive eschatological reality, is thus communicated to men. The community of the faithful redeemed by the blood of Christ and incorporated in him, is progressively led by means of the sacraments toward transfiguration and divinization. Herein lies the profound life and reality of our Churches. It is here that there is effected the mysterious communion that unites them, mysterious yet real and operative like every work of God.

In both East and West, the activating of these gifts, the development of the sacramental life of the Church, and the forms taken by this common faith, have been diverse, rich and complementary in their variety.

This sacramental reality which gives us life is the basis of the firm relations which exist between our Churches. It gives consistency to the dialogue—so rich in hope—that is now opening up. It should make it possible for us to tackle with Christian realism, and to clarify once for all, all the points which are still a source of difficulty, and which keep us from concelebrating together the Holy Eucharist. It is centered in the very heart of this mystery, at the central point where the multiplicity and variety that is visible on the surface, are taken up in unity. It is there, in this light, that we shall discover and recognize one another as true brothers; that we shall recognize and discover that our Churches are truly sister Churches. In view of this, we consider the work being done in both our Churches by the technical commissions responsible for preparing the theological dialogue as most important. And since the next phase of preparation of the dialogue must necessarily be co-ordinated, we are glad that it has already proved possible to appoint two sub-commissions that will meet to put this work of co-ordination into effect. It is urgent that we put an end once and for all to these differences inherited from the past.

For all these reasons, Your Holiness, we are profoundly glad to be here and to pray together to the Lord, certain that our common prayer is an echo, in us, of the prayer that Christ addressed to the Father for the Church: "That they may be one, that the world may believe" (Jn. 17:21). That the world may believe. This world full of tensions and of weariness, of enmity and irresponsibility, of violence and lassitude, of injustice and also of hope ... this world of ours is waiting for someone to come to free it and change it; to make of it a single family living in peace and love. The Church must bear witness by its unity and the quality of its fraternal life, for this is the work of the Lord. May he be with us.

I have the honor, Your Holiness, of conveying a personal message from the Holy Father, Pope Paul VI.

* * *

Then the Cardinal read aloud the message from Pope Paul to the Patriarch.

2) *Message from Pope Paul to the Patriarch*

To His Holiness Demetrios
Archbishop of Constantinople
Ecumenical Patriarch

In celebrating by the tomb of Peter the feast of his brother Andrew, our thoughts turn to you, dear Brother, and our fraternal charity is expressed in a fervent prayer for your intentions and for the faithful of your Church. This spiritual encounter in prayer between the Churches of Rome and Constantinople is manifested by the presence among you of our brother Cardinal John Willebrands and those who accompany him. He brings you our kiss of peace, a sign of the fraternity which must exist and grow deeper between our two Churches.

During these last few weeks which have marked the tenth anniversary of the visit your great predecessor made to us, how could one fail to recall the beautiful icon that he sent us as a souvenir of our meeting on the Mount of Olives: Peter and Andrew embracing with the blessing of Christ the Lord? This gesture betokens the programme to be carried out through an ever greater sharing in the truth, until the day comes—so greatly longed for—when the bishop of Rome and the bishop of Constantinople will be able to exchange this kiss of peace in the concelebration of the most Holy Eucharist. For this it is necessary that the obstacles that still exist between us should be surmounted. We hope that the commissions we have established will be able—without delay, but with prudence—to coordinate their efforts so that the theological dialogue may begin which should allow us to resolve our last remaining differences.

During these days, we ask the Holy Spirit with special fervor to help us go forward together, with prudent courage, along this path, guided by His light and animated by His strength.

On this unity depends the credibility of the witness we have to give to Christ in the world today. This witness is our constant preoccupation. In this spirit the Synod of Bishops which has just ended has attempted to clarify what means are apt to ensure the Christian formation of the young with a view to helping them become witnesses to Christ among their fellowmen. We therefore express to you once again our firm resolve to do everything possible to achieve this unity, that "the world may believe" (Jn. 17:21).

Assuring you, beloved and venerable Brother, of our deep fraternal charity,

Paulus PP. VI

From the Vatican, dated 24 November, 1977.

3) *Speech of His Holiness Patriarch Demetrios*

Your Eminence, Brother in Christ, Cardinal John Wille-brands, archbishop and president of the Vatican Secretariat for Promoting Christian Unity, and you, his fellow-workers and collaborators,

God has willed that the patronal feasts of our two Churches should be blessed each year by these invaluable reciprocal visits. A year has already passed since the idea was first suggested here. Subsequently, it was decided by both sides to have this regular annual exchange of visits.

And so, after the visit to Rome of our representatives last June, on the occasion of the commemoration of SS Peter and Paul, the chief Apostles, today we are receiving in this place, in the new Rome, in the patriarchal see of this city, on the annual feast of Saint Andrew, Saint Peter's brother, the visit of the venerable delegation of His Holiness the Pope of Rome.

We rejoice at these reciprocal visits. We greet your presence among us as a special grace of God, as a special joy for our Church, and as a force and an encouragement for the faithful.

And your visit, brothers, is also intended, among other things, to underline the major fact of this year. That is, that ten years have passed since the day when the Lord led to this city our elder Brother, the first bishop of Christendom, in an official visit to our predecessor of venerated memory, the much-lamented Patriarch Athenagoras, as he had guided the steps of the Patriarch towards ancient Rome, "which presides in charity." History has already inscribed in indelible pages— as was long due—this event which has brought to an end and sealed a cycle of almost a thousand years of separation between East and West.

May God be glorified for all He has disposed in our favor. Our response to all this is twofold.

On the one hand, it is in a spirit of esteem and gratitude that we shall soon send our delegation to Rome, as a fraternal response to the precious message of His Holiness, received from the hands of Your Eminence. We are convinced that these regular meetings in which we can see each other and talk, rather than relations conducted by "pen and ink," to quote the Apostle John (3 Jn. 13-14), not only profoundly touch our hearts, but become so many stones in the construction of the edifice of the reconciliation and unity of our Churches.

On the other hand, taking the opportunity of the presence among us of you who are the untiring artisans of unity among Christians, you who make a decisive contribution to its realization, we should like to express our thoughts about the sacred cause of the theological dialogue between our two Churches.

Well-beloved brothers in the Lord:

The two expert commissions composed of theologians and appointed to prepare the theological dialogue, are already in full activity. Last year, on this same day, we announced the pan-orthodox decision regarding the immediate start of the work of the inter-orthodox commission. At the same time, on the part of ancient Rome there was the announcement of the setting up of a similar expert commission, composed of Roman Catholic theologians, and the first results of its plenary session were communicated. During those days, you and the members of our synodal commission here had the occasion to inform each other of all this. As for the inter-orthodox expert theological commission which has already held two meetings this year, it has made considerable progress in what concerns the methodology and the problems involved in dialogue. It is the doctrine on the sacraments which has been chosen as the first and principal subject for this phase in the dialogue.

We consider this choice to have been a happy one. There is no doubt that it is very prudent to lay down the main lines of the problems that arise in the various phases of dialogue. The last thing we want is that the discussions should be held to no purpose. On the contrary, the preparation of the dialogue must be serious, the fruit of reflection; and it must be based on concrete data. It is therefore without hesitation that we say here that the domain of the sacraments offers a large and favorable field for fruitful dialogue.

We say this in view of the two following basic facts:

Firstly, since we have the same sacraments, that is to say, the same baptism, the same Eucharist, the same priesthood in an uninterrupted apostolic ordination; and also we share the principal doctrinal points regarding the other sacraments, confirmation, marriage, confession, and the anointing of the sick, all of which are united in the unique and incontestable mystery of the Church, the One Body of Christ, he who is the one "who offers and is offered, who receives and is distributed, Christ our true God . . . ;" since we have in common, that is, all the deposit of the faith in this field, we must explore together through a constructive dialogue the ways to our unity in Christ.

We say with conviction that our theological dialogue should start and then develop on these points that we share and not on themes that divide our Churches. It is a different matter, to examine and define the theological and practical differences affecting our common doctrine on the sacraments. We acknowledge the variety which exists in this domain, often of long standing, a variety that is also called diversity or plurality. But we say without any reservation that this does not in any way harm the essence of dialogue; that on the contrary, it builds up the unity which we are seeking, and which we shall continue to seek, within diversity, in the liturgical, pastoral, historical, and canonical fields. Unity must not be an exact resemblance or a rigid uniformity of form and expression, but rather an identity in faith, in teaching, in grace and in belief in Christ, with full respect for the traditional institutions of our Churches, institutions to which history and theology bear witness.

We should like to underline this once again: in the whole of this new phase in the dialogue, which is so full of hope, our Churches must not get stuck in discussions on those subjects that have previously led the two parties to impasses and confrontations. On the contrary, with honesty, fidelity to the truth, and full theological integrity, we must seek and find new, more positive approaches to revealed truth, which in itself is one and indivisible.

We shall do this in our theological dialogue. Without ignoring the differences that have existed for so long, and without failing to appreciate, in a true light, all that was the object of discussion in the past, however fruitless this may have been, we shall conduct our dialogue primarily in a positive and constructive manner, with the fear of God and the love of Christ.

If in order to do this, and to overcome the difficulties that have accumulated—historical, psychological, or others—a special effort and courage in decision-making are required from one side or the other we feel that none of us should any longer neglect this or any effort required.

Today both East and West are living through new realities that arouse large aspirations and ecumenical hopes, new theological tendencies and directions centered on the concept of mutual understanding, reciprocal knowledge, and acceptance of one another. What seemed out of the question only a short time ago, has in our days become a reality; what was once unforeseen, men now find the courage to put into effect, and this is true even of those who are not Christians. What about us Christians, shall we be content with appearing to others to be doing nothing? Certainly not. If we were content to keep to yesterday's methods, our dialogue would be in vain, and vain would be our preaching, and hollow our homilies on reconciliation, unity and ecumenism.

These are the ideas, my brothers, which we wished to put forward today. May the Lord give his blessing to all that will follow.

With these thoughts in our minds and hearts, thoughts that carry such hopes, in this solemn moment we spiritually embrace the chief Shepherd of Ancient Rome, our brother Pope Paul VI, beloved in Christ and in his Church. We salute you with love and esteem, you his worthy representatives, as we recall the words of the prophet Isaiah: "How beautiful on the mountains, are the feet of one who brings good news, who heralds peace, brings happiness, proclaims salvation" (Is. 52:7).

2. Visit of Metropolitan Meliton at Rome: December 7, 1977

On December 7th, the anniversary of the fraternal act by which the Churches of Rome and Constantinople, at the conclusion of Vatican II (1965) proceeded to remove their (mutual) excommunications, Meliton, the Metropolitan of Chalcedon and Dean of the Holy Synod of the Ecumenical Patriarchate, went on a visit to Rome and was received by the Holy Father.

In the name of Patriarch Demetrios, the Metropolitan gave the Holy Father a lamp taken from the private chapel of the Ecumenical Patriarch. The motive and symbolic meaning of this gift are inscribed on either side of the silver plaque:

On the front is written: "Men light a lamp and put it on the lamp-stand where it shines for everyone in the house" (Mt. 5:15).

On the back: "To the Holy Brother of Rome Paul VI, Demetrios of Constantinople, on the occasion of his 80th birthday and in token of the fact that truly 'it shines for everyone in the house.' "

1. *During the audience, the Metropolitan read the following message from Patriarch Demetrios:*

To His Holiness Pope Paul VI, Bishop of Ancient Rome, Demetrios Bishop of Constantinople, Greeting in the Lord.

We have just received at our Holy See the delegation of your beloved Holiness presided over by your worthy representative, His Eminence Cardinal John Willebrands, who, under the inspiration and direction of Your Holiness, expresses perfectly the will of the Holy Roman Catholic Church for Christian unity in general and, more especially, your desire and will that this holy and great cause of Christian unity should be founded on the solid ecclesiological unity of the Western and Eastern Churches.

Replying with the greatest joy to the very holy message addressed by Your Holiness from the See of the Apostle Peter to this See of his brother the Apostle Andrew—a message which deeply moved ourself and the Church of Constantinople because of its important content—we have charged the dean of our holy and sacred Synod, the Most Eminent Metropolitan of Chalcedon, our beloved and esteemed brother in Christ, Msgr. Meliton, to visit Your Holiness in a special mission for this purpose on our behalf and to express to Your Holiness and your very Holy Roman Catholic Church in the first place our thanks and those of our very holy Church, for the continuation of the dialogue of charity in all sincere and brotherly understanding as well as the preparation, with painstaking care on both sides, of the theological dialogue between the two Churches; also, but at the same time, our assurance that we are ready to pull down all walls erected between us during the centuries, in order to be able to communicate together in the body and the blood of the Lord in a common Holy Eucharist.

With this wish we send Your Holiness, as a humble expression of love, brotherly honor and our gratitude to your venerated person as the first Bishop of Christendom in the world, a lamp from our private patriarchal chapel, so that it may be placed in your private chapel, as a sign of the fact that "the light of Christ gives light to all."

Addressing that in all love and honor to Your Holiness on the occasion of your eightieth birthday, the twelfth anniversary of the removal of the anathemas between our two Churches and the tenth anniversary of the visit of our predecessor of eternal memory, Patriarch Athenagoras, to Your Holiness and Your Very Holy Church, we beg the Lord to bestow on Your Holiness, beloved by us, long life in constant good health, and on the Church an ever greater testimony that we are all one in Christ our only Lord.

The beloved brother of Your very Venerable Holiness
Demetrios of Constantinople

2. *The Pope replied to the reading of the message with the following words of thanks and good wishes.*

Your Eminence,

In the liturgical period of Advent, when the bracing wind of messianic hope blows over the Christian Churches, and on this anniversary of the historic day of December 7, 1965, your visit takes on its whole significance! We thank God for these regular brotherly meetings between our Churches, and we congratulate Your Eminence on being, on your side, a convinced architect of them.

Yes, slowly but surely, our communities are moving toward complete meeting. At this moment, the formation of an Orthodox sub-commission charged with contacting the similar Catholic sub-commission, with a view to arriving at the creation of a mixed commission for theological dialogue, is a step forward which we consider very important. And the dialogue between our Churches, based on the sacramental reality itself, benefits from a solid foundation which holds out the hope of overcoming the difficulties which do not yet permit a concelebration of the Eucharist.

We ask you to express to His Holiness the Ecumenical Patriarch Demetrios I our feelings of brotherly affection and our invincible hope in the success of our joint efforts, humble and loyal, patient and repeated. May the Spirit of unity and holiness renew constantly the hearts of the pastors and faithful of the Orthodox and Catholic communities, and prepare them more and more for complete and definitive reconciliation "so that the world may believe"!

3. *Interview given to Vatican Radio by Meliton, Metropolitan of Chalcedon.*

D. Immediately after the audience with the Holy Father, Metropolitan Meliton of Chalcedon, the Dean of the Holy Synod of Constantinople, gave over Radio Vatican the following impression of his meeting with Paul VI.

R. My impressions of this audience which I have had with His Holiness Paul VI are excellent. I found him rejuvenated in spirit, ever ready to serve the Church and the cause of the unity of Christians. I had the privilege of examining, with His Holiness, the whole panorama of the relations between

the Catholic and Orthodox Churches, and together we saw
what great progress has been made.

D. Would you just touch on the motive for this meeting with
the Pope?

R. I am here as a special envoy of His Holiness the Ecumenical Patriarch Demetrios, to consign a special message from
him in reply to the message sent by Cardinal Willebrands
on November 30, last. The significance of my visit to Rome
today, December 7, is rather special since it was twelve
years ago, on December 7, 1965, that I personally received
from the Pontiff the Pontifical Brief removing the mutual
excommunication between the two Churches of Rome and
Constantinople.

D. The Christian world prays for unity. From your experience,
what hopes are there for the realization of this ecumenical
aspiration?

R. We have great hopes, based on what has already been
accomplished. As regards relations between the Catholic
and Orthodox Churches, it can be said that we have now
entered a most important phase. As you know, there have
been set up two theological commissions, one Roman
Catholic, the other inter-orthodox, attended by all local
Orthodox Churches. These two commissions are preparing
the theological dialogue between the two Churches. The
latest progress made consists in the fact that each commission has appointed a sub-committee, and that these two
sub-committees will hold a meeting next March in order to
co-ordinate the work of preparing the theological dialogue.